your
WEDDING

your
WAY

your
WEDDING
your
WAY

Break with Tradition and Create a
One-of-a-Kind Celebration
You'll Never Forget!

Sharon Naylor

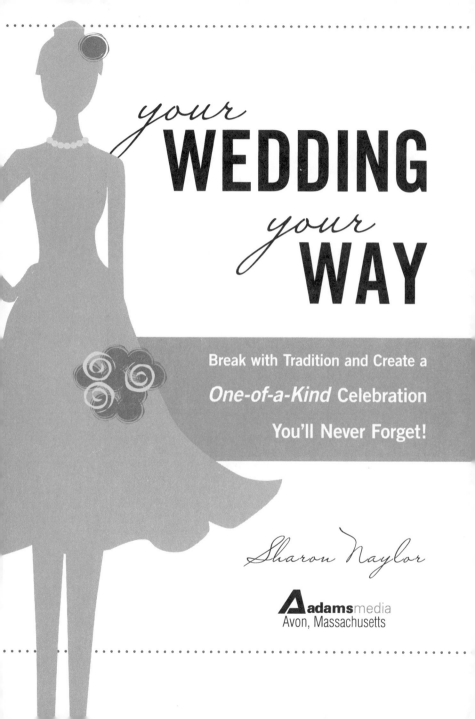

A **adams**media
Avon, Massachusetts

Published by
Adams Media, a division of F+W Media, Inc.
57 Littlefield Street, Avon, MA 02322. U.S.A.
www.adamsmedia.com

ISBN-10: 1-60550-104-2
ISBN-13: 978-1-60550-104-8

Printed in the United States of America.

10 9 8 7 6 5 4 3 2 1

Library of Congress Cataloging-in-Publication Data
is available from the publisher.

This publication is designed to provide accurate and authoritative information with
regard to the subject matter covered. It is sold with the understanding that the publisher is not engaged in rendering legal, accounting, or other professional advice. If
legal advice or other expert assistance is required, the services of a competent professional person should be sought.
—From a *Declaration of Principles* jointly adopted by a Committee of the American
Bar Association and a Committee of Publishers and Associations

Many of the designations used by manufacturers and sellers to distinguish their prod-
uct are claimed as trademarks. Where those designations appear in this book and
Adams Media was aware of a trademark claim, the designations have been printed
with initial capital letters.

This book is available at quantity discounts for bulk purchases.
For information, please call 1-800-289-0963.

For my husband, Joe

ACKNOWLEDGMENTS

Big hugs of thanks and immense respect for my editor and shooting star, Katrina Schroeder, for bringing me this wonderful opportunity to help *you* plan your wedding your way. Katrina has always been such an inspiring editor, and I'm thrilled to partner with her once again in this immensely joyous wedding arena.

My thanks and bows to the feet of my illustrious agent, Meredith Bernstein, who has leaped over the line into my family as well as my heart and, like any good mentor, has truly had my back on all occasions.

I'm filled with happiness over the opportunities I've had to work with some of the best media masters out there, including Crys Stewart and Stacie Francombe at Get Married, Anja Winnika and Jordana Starr at "I Do! With The Knot," Lauren Gould at Martha Stewart Living on Sirius Satellite Radio, the lovely and festive Sasha Souza, and my dear friends Ashley Diamond and Audra Lowe at Better.tv. You ladies make it fabulous to face the cameras!

And to my colleagues at ABC, ISES, and HSMAI, thank you for the world of education you provide to all of our association members and for your willingness to share stories and tips with my readers.

And to my Joe, who joined me in planning *our wedding our way.* You are a dream come true.

CONTENTS

INTRODUCTION

Many recent brides and grooms complain that their dream wedding—the day that they put more than $20,000 into—had them running at a frantic pace with nonstop photo sessions and timed-to-the-minute "musts" (like the bouquet toss and cutting the cake), followed by more photo sessions. They didn't get any time to spend with friends who flew in for their big day. They didn't even get a chance to *eat*. They didn't get to have fun. The day may have been beautiful, but it wasn't a truly beautiful experience for *them*. Well, I don't want you and your fiancé saying that about *your* wedding. I'm going to show you how to break with tradition and make this day *your* day—absent all of the musts and shoulds you feel pressured to include. I'm going to put the fun back into your wedding and give you more quality time to spend with the friends and loved ones you haven't seen in years.

You'll find out how to choose which traditions you want to break (or bend just a little); how to style your dream theme wedding; and how to break the news to your parents, your in-laws, and your grandparents that you're not having the cookie-cutter wedding *they* may be dreaming about.

Your first dance might be a tango, and your wedding cake might be a big Boston cream pie instead of a five-tiered iced bridal cake. This is your wedding, your way . . . and it's going to be perfect because it'll be exactly how *you two* want it!

Part One

THE BASICS

Planning a wedding begins at Step One, with the setting of the fundamentals—the date, time, season, formality, and other factors that will determine many of the big decisions. All those big decisions feed into the details, from largest down to the smallest. Your wish to have your wedding your way makes *your* Step One quite a bit different . . . and challenging.

Step One is where you decide how you wish to break with tradition, and to what degree, so that your wedding reflects *you* and not what everyone else wants. You essentially have a blank slate before you, which is the essence of not following cliché wedding traditions, and you'll either be excited about the possibilities or overwhelmed about just how much responsibility you have to design a personalized wedding that's going to be the best celebration ever.

Take plenty of time to work through the next chapters together, and by the time you're finished with this part, you'll be well on your way to a personalized wedding plan.

CHAPTER 1

Breaking with Tradition

Everyone has something to say about your wedding. *But that's how things are done!* and *But it's tradition in our family!* and *What will people think?* have rung in the ears of many brides and grooms, as parents push their own agendas or try to prevent "making a mistake with your wedding." You've probably heard plenty of stories from your friends—or watched a sibling go through torture with her own wedding plans—as battles unfold, guilt trips are lobbed like grenades, feelings are hurt, and the wedding becomes a huge, hurtful tug-of-war that causes *both* sides of the family to think less of one another. And there are the poor bride and groom, lost in the chaos, as their initial blissful sigh of "I can't wait for this wedding" turns into "I can't wait for this wedding to be *over*." All because of a group struggle over tradition.

This struggle starts innocently enough: you wish to have your wedding, your way.

Part of your vision, if you're like most brides and grooms these days, may include breaking with tradition. The break may be in small ways, such as chopping some religious wording out of your ceremony, or in big ways, such as discarding the entire traditional wedding in favor of a fun theme wedding, or a casual wedding. You're not the couple who wants a cookie-cutter wedding that looks, sounds, and tastes like every other wedding in the family. No carbon copies of your friends' weddings for you. You don't subscribe to the musts, and shoulds of wedding world, since your world is nothing like the decades-old society that *created* the vast majority of wedding "rules." You're modern and independent, and you plan to make your wedding reflect who you are as a couple. When you think about traditions like tossing the bouquet to the single women, or even wearing a white wedding dress, you cringe. After all, those traditions were built from the beliefs of a society you don't live in.

How Traditions Originated

Many wedding traditions come from agrarian societies of ancient times, where the bride was "given" to the groom's family, the white dress meant virginity, the cake meant fertility, and the bridesmaids dressed like the bride to confuse evil spirits that might whisk her away. The groom stood to the right of the bride so that his right hand would be free to grab his sword to fend off marauders who also wanted to steal the bride. From the Victorian era, we got bridal bouquets, whose scents (mostly herbs) were to hide the stench of an unclean society, or also to ward off those evil spirits. Boy, there were a lot of evil spirits and bride-stealing bands of miscreants out there in those days! Our society carries these traditions through because of the mentality of superstition that still remains, especially in the minds of parents. Though we've changed some of the traditions into good-luck rituals and added modern flavors and designs to the basic template of the traditional wedding, many of those ancient ideas still appear.

If you're not bound by Old World belief systems, you're probably not going to want to be bound by Old World traditions. What fun is that?

Your Parents' Take on Weddings

Now let's look at another angle of breaking with tradition. You don't want the wedding your parents had—but they probably want that wedding for you. They may want the church wedding. The white dress. The sit-down dinner. That's how it's done in their experience of weddings *and* from their memories of what the wedding industry offered by way of catering and décor. They only have their own frame of reference, which probably hasn't been exposed much to the way things are now. Thus, the battles described at the start of this chapter. In the next chapter, we'll get into handling your parents in detail.

How Many Weddings Are Nontraditional?

So how common are these personalized, break-with-tradition weddings? Is it really a growing trend? According to TheWedding Report.com, only about half of today's weddings are traditional. Here's how the current surveys report wedding styles:

TYPE OF WEDDING PLANNED

Traditional	51%
Casual	19%
Formal	13%
Unique	10%
Extravagant	2%
Theme	3%
Other	2%

Printed courtesy of TheWeddingReport.com

Looking at these numbers, you might think, "Excellent! Only 3 percent of weddings are theme based, so that's going to make ours really stand out!" I include this survey report here not to sway you toward any particular style of wedding—I'm here to help you plan your wedding your way, after all!—but just to let you know what's going on in the wedding world you're about to enter. Remember, just as many couples say "Other" as say "Extravagant," so you're in good company if you too want the freedom to choose "Other"!

Why Do You Want What You Want?

First, let's figure out why you want to break with tradition. No important task can be achieved well unless you truly understand the *values* within you that guide your wish list. You might say, "I want to do something really different," but considering your wedding plans involve so many additional people, such as friends and family—maybe some of them helping to pay for the big day—it's wise to be able to explain *why* you're gravitating toward a nontraditional wedding style. You *will* be questioned on it, by family members and by the vendors who make it their own personal goal to bring your wishes to life. Once *you* understand why you want to tweak or break certain traditions for your big day, you can then explain it perfectly to those around you . . . leading to a much clearer and much more peaceful planning process because others "get you."

So let's explore the various values that could be making you gravitate toward "different." Which of the following factors ring true to you? Feel free to check off more than one, since most brides say that multiple values apply for them. It's rarely just one thing.

○ Religion is not a big part of your life, so you would find it unsettling to make it a big part of your wedding.

○ You live a "green" lifestyle and would like your values reflected in your wedding plans.

○ You don't want the same wedding everyone else has had, just with different colored flowers and a different design of wedding cake.

○ You *know* that unique weddings are a lot of fun. You've been to some terrific ones, and you had a blast.

○ You want to add more personalized elements to your wedding than traditional models allow, such as current cultural themes and humor that reflects your relationship.

○ You want plenty of children in attendance at your wedding, since your extended family is so very important to you. You wouldn't dream of leaving all the kids off the list.

○ You want your friends and family to have a unique wedding experience, since so many of them are traveling so far to attend your big day. They deserve more than a cookie-cutter wedding experience.

○ You've already done the traditional wedding thing for your first marriage, or your groom has, and you want to do something different.

○ You're not pretentious, and you don't want a lavish display of wealth and expense at the wedding. The simpler, the better.

○ You don't want anyone telling you how to plan your day. This includes parents, the in-laws, and your wedding vendors.

○ Your wedding ideas would cost far less than those involved with a traditional wedding.

○ You want the once-in-a-lifetime experience of custom-designing your big celebration, and having wedding experts bring your ideas, sketches, and dreams to life.

○ You want this to be fun!

What are your additional factors? List them here:

_____

_____

_____

_____

_____

> **"**I've always felt that if I had a traditional, white wedding that it would feel like I cut-and-pasted myself into someone else's wedding picture. It's just not my style. I'm thinking about a Shakespearean fantasy wedding set in the woods, like *A Midsummer Night's Dream*, with me in a gossamer dress and flowers in my hair, and my groom in a Shakespearean costume, a massive feast, and lots of wine as the sun sets and we have thousands of tiny lights in the trees. The only aisle I want to walk down would be the path between the trees. **"** — *Leslie*, **bride-to-be**

How Far Do You Want to Take It?

Your next decision is how far you want go in breaking with tradition. Would you like a traditional wedding with just a few elements tweaked to reflect your values and your relationship?

For many brides and grooms, just being able to change the existing traditional elements—such as lighting a larger, antique, decorative oil lamp instead of lighting a unity taper candle—is enough creativity and difference. And for other couples, a dream wedding would take place on Halloween—they'd dress as ghost bride and groom, and all of their guests would wear creative costumes. Everyone would drink red "blood" martinis, and munch on sushi "eyeballs" as they dance all night to Halloween-themed music and get their fortunes read by a professional psychic. They get married, and their guests get to enjoy picking out what to wear for the big day. It would be unlike any other wedding the guests have ever attended. Both of these breaks with tradition are wonderful because they reflect what the couple wants.

As you consider the question of tradition breaking, flip ahead to Chapters 3 and 4 to discover a list of creative twists to traditional wedding elements and discuss them together. You may find that incorporating a few of these simple and fun tweaks to your wedding plans fulfills your need to be different from the crowd and lets you custom-design your day to a nonthreatening degree. Perhaps just a few elements are all you'll need to plan your way.

> "My parents would freak out if we wanted to plan a Halloween theme wedding! They look so sour when they see theme weddings on television shows, so I know it would be inviting a huge mess of conflict if we went *that* far in personalizing our day. We'll go with the Moderation Plan and just change lots of things within the standard wedding concept." — *Victoria*, **bride-to-be**

In Chapter 4 you'll get more in-depth on how and where you'd like to break tradition, *and in Chapter 2 you'll discover the number one secret step to making your wedding different from everyone else's.* In addition, one very important factor is that you *both* have to fall in love with each other's requests to break with tradition. Agree now to honor each other's preferences and gut reactions to fun, in-the-moment inspiration. The last thing you want is a wedding that's been turned into a talent show by your ultra-creative partner, to the point where guests ask themselves "How much attention do these people need?" Yes, it's romantic for the groom to sing to you, but do you really need his high school garage band to reunite at your wedding reception? Save that for their twentieth class reunion, where they would be far better appreciated. Remember—and you'll read this again later in the book—any idea can be used for *other* events taking place during the wedding weekend, or for other parties, such as birthday celebrations or anniversary parties.

Now before we move into the next step—breaking the news to your parents and grandparents that you will *not* be having the traditional wedding of *their* dreams—let's first make sure you're 100 percent ready to talk with them. That means spending a lot of time discussing between the two of you exactly what you want your wedding to be like—which traditions you want to embrace, which you want to tweak or do away with—and building your priority list of what's most important to you for your big day.

Each of these issues is vitally important for you to agree upon and be very clear about each other's wishes for so that you can approach your parents and grandparents as a united front with clear communication. When you're completely in synch with each other, there's no room for confusion when parents start making *their* requests and demands. Which they'll likely start doing immediately. So this is a task you have to get on right now. With no gray areas between you, there's little threat that you or your groom will agree to something the parents want simply because it wasn't a topic you talked about. And make it a promise that if a parent does make a request, you'll answer with "Let me talk to (partner) about that first. We're making all decisions together."

This way, there's no conflict about who promised what to whom, no accusations of betrayal or going behind your back—all very common problems when a wedding couple doesn't have their wedding style and details discussed thoroughly before parents are invited into the circle.

Take some time now to *write down* exactly what you both want for the wedding, pull some images out of magazines or print them from wedding websites, and start compiling your wedding research while it's still just the two of you planning. You'll need this information for upcoming steps. There's no better way to have your wedding your way than to *start* in an organized and clear manner. Plus, it's just more fun this way—which is what you're aiming for. Imagine the chaos if you approached parents without any vision of your own wedding! They'd have far more power to plan it their way. Read on for insights and an approach plan for letting parents and grandparents—who can sometimes be just as influential, persuasive, and demanding as parents—know that you're going to break with tradition in plenty of ways so that your wedding reflects *you* as a couple.

CHAPTER 2

How to Decide What You Both Want for Your Wedding Day

You *both* have to be in agreement on the various ways you will create your wedding your way. The best way to get in agreement is to talk about everything. Here's a little quiz to get the discussion started. Take this quiz together, and use different-colored pens to check off your answers and make additional notes. Don't worry if you're not in total agreement right now—few wedding couples are at this stage. You've already gone through the checklist in the introduction about *why* you'd like to have a nontraditional wedding, and now you're getting in a little deeper.

1. **How comfortable are you when you're at formal celebrations, such as black-tie weddings and dress-up events?**
   a **Very comfortable.** I love getting dressed up, looking my best, and enjoying "the good life" at formal weddings.
   b. **Somewhat comfortable.** Being in high heels or a suit is fine for the first few hours, but then I'd rather be home in pajamas, watching television.

   c. **I hate it.** Nothing's worse than being forced to wear high heels or a suit just because someone wants everyone to look good in their pictures.

2. **What's the best location for your wedding?**

   a. Right here in our hometown, which is going to be gorgeous at the time of year we're getting married, and it's close for all our guests to get to.

   b. It would be dreamy if we could get married at our favorite vacation destination that we go to every year, get married on the beach at sunset, and have foods from our favorite restaurants there.

   c. Someplace we've never been before, like our dream destination of Hawaii. And to bring everyone else with us? That would be amazing.

   d. Someplace not in our hometown, but also not a five-hour flight away, either.

3. **How do you feel about an outdoor wedding?**

   a. It's perfect! Nothing says "wedding" more than gorgeous scenery, everyone in the gardens, surrounded by flowers.

   b. I'd be too worried about the weather and bugs ruining the day.

   c. I'm all for it if the place we book has an indoor ballroom we could move into if it rains.

   d. I've always hated outdoor parties. Who wants to bring sunblock to a wedding and sweat through her dress?

4. **What is the worst part of a traditional wedding?**

   a. Having the same old food.

   b. Having the same old music.

   c. It's expensive no matter how you plan it.

   d. Having to go by the rules of a church or reception hall.

5. **How important is it for you to invite *everyone* you know to the wedding?**
    a. Very important. It wouldn't be a wedding without all our relatives and their kids, and all our friends there.
    b. Not too important. I'd be happy with just a small circle of close relatives and friends.
    c. I really don't care, as long as we get married.

6. **How do you feel about a wedding being *funny,* having laugh-out-loud moments?**
    a. That makes it great! Our guests would love it, so we're going to insert some humor in the ceremony and in the emcee's wording at the reception.
    b. That would offend our parents and other relatives.
    c. I think weddings should be solemn and serious—funny toasts and the like should be done at the rehearsal dinner only.
    d. We're all for it if any toast-makers want to be funny, but we're not going to plan special comedy moments for our big day.

You've just discussed some basic, fundamental issues as you cocreate your personalized wedding day. These questions may have even sent you off on tangents, discussing your thoughts and suggestions for your dream-wedding day, planned your way! Notice there's no "scoring," no "if you circled mostly B, then . . ." rules. This exercise was just to get the discussion on the table. Take notes on every inspiration that arises as you work through this section. Some ideas will work and some won't, but that's the creative process.

What Are Your Common Passions?

A great many personalized or theme weddings are built around a couple's shared interests. Their passion for wine, for instance, becomes the basis for their Tuscan-inspired wedding. Their passion for Latin dancing and culture naturally inspires a Latin-themed wedding with fabulous music and a packed dance floor, and even the bride's gown may have a Latin flair. Add a red rose behind her ear, and she's perfectly accessorized for a day that's truly *her*.

The activities and interests you share make your wedding *you*.

In this section, you'll look at all the lifestyle activities and interests you share, to find the large and small ways you can incorporate them into your day. And keep in mind that a shared interest doesn't have to become the overall theme of your day. It could be an addition to your menu, a choice for one of your cocktail party stations, or a block of songs played during the dinner hour. As you work through this area, color-code for each idea to help you organize yourself. You might highlight or circle an idea in pink if it's ideal for the cocktail party, in blue if it works for your reception, red if it's perfect for an after-party or the morning-after breakfast.

Remember, you get to create themes for several different events during your wedding weekend, so you have lots of room to play here.

CULTURAL INTERESTS

Which cultures fascinate and inspire you? Are there any regions of the world you've always wanted to visit, but have not yet been able to? Would you like to design your wedding's theme to reflect a Moroccan culture, a Far East land of intrigue, or a recreation of the land of your family's ancestors? Some of the top cultural wedding themes are connected to the couple's heritage, *but that's not a rule!* Since we are a global society, you can design your wedding to be an international, exotic adventure that brings you and your guests to India, Korea, the Seychelles, Ireland, any-where on the map.

CULINARY INTERESTS

We're also a nation of foodies, with a love of themed menus pre-pared for us on television by the Food Network's top gourmands and sommeliers. If you're looking for the perfect theme wedding to reflect you, you might need to look no further than the culinary favorites on your cookbook shelf, or the ingredients in your kitchen pantry. You might design a New Orleans–style wedding with jam-balaya, shrimp étouffée, beignets, and a lineup of authentic menu items that guests will love because they haven't had them at every other wedding they've attended. You incorporate your favorite cui-sine, and your guests get transported to The Big Easy.

You could also consider French, Italian, hot and trendy fusion foods such as Japanese and Cuban, or Vietnamese—there's a world's worth of culinary treasures available to you. You can cre-ate an international travel–themed wedding, giving your guests passports to have stamped at each food station, with extra stamps if they try the most unique, authentic, spiciest, or most unusual food items. You'll then turn your wedding into a culinary adventure!

YOUR FAVORITE HOLIDAYS

An October wedding presents the opportunity for costumed fun if you plan a Halloween wedding with all your guests invited to wear their choice of Halloween get-up, and a decor designed as a haunted house. The big new trend in personalized weddings that break with tradition is to give guests an experience unlike any they get in their everyday lives, and since Halloween is a favorite holiday for many guests of all ages, it's no wonder this is one of the top holiday-themed weddings. Menu items can be designed to look like worms (capellini) and eyeballs (deviled eggs or sushi), or can include actual frog legs and other delicacies that work with a creepy theme. You can present your bouquet to the guest with the greatest costume rather than throwing it to a throng of single women guests. Add spooky lighting and black lights, lots of cobwebs, and animatronic Halloween zombies at the doors, not to mention outdoor décor such as luminarias and a dessert buffet that's filled with trick-or-treat candies, and you have a great Halloween theme wedding.

For a New Year's Eve wedding, design your space like a nightclub. Have lots of flashing lights and use silver metallic streamers surrounding silver champagne buckets and champagne bottles as the centerpieces of your tables. Give out kitschy New Year's items from the craft store to your guests, such as noisemakers and those oversized glasses with the new year's numerals on them. And concoct colorful drinks with theme names such as "Baby New Year Banana Coladas" and "Midnight Kiss Martinis." Play the top music hits of the calendar year. Have big-screen television monitors everywhere, showing the New York City Times Square New Year's celebration, complete with celebrity musical performances. Set out cards at each table on which guests can record their New Year's resolutions to share with friends and family. Then serve breakfast in the wee hours after you've all rung in the new year with plenty of drinks and dancing. The New Year's wedding is one of the most popular holiday-themed weddings, since many adults say they're usually at home in their pajamas on this holiday, wishing they were at a fun bash. You can now fulfill their wishes with your New Year's wedding.

MUSIC STYLES

Did the two of you meet or become close due to a shared love of a style of music? If that style was jazz, you could design your wedding to look, sound, and feel like an upscale jazz club, with live performers, dim lighting, and pinlights set on each guest table. Play the standards, both classic and new, for a night of dancing and music appreciation that suits a crowd that appreciates fine cuisine, great drinks, and entertainment that is as far from The Chicken Dance as you can get. If that favorite band is too pricey or hard to reach, consider a cover band. Or if you don't want to overdo it with the jazz music, ask your band if they can play 50 percent jazz music and 50 percent other styles of music.

FAVORITE ERA IN TIME

What era in history most appeals to you? Some couples love the 1940s for their USO flavor and big band swing. Guests can do the Lindy, and your bridesmaids can wear their hair in Andrews Sisters styles with bright red lipstick and back-seam stockings. A 1980s-era wedding allows you to play the music from what might be your favorite time in history, and television monitors on the walls can play *The Breakfast Club* and your other favorite 1980s movies. Have your servers dress up like Madonna in her lace gloves period, with the silver crosses and super-teased hair, and a Boy George impersonator can be the bartender. There are so many options for naming things after 1980s iconic pop culture references (Duran Duran's "Hungry Like the Wolf" buffet bar comes to mind), and of course you can be dressed *Pretty in Pink* for your reception costume change if you'd like.

Going further back in time, think about a 1920s speakeasy theme, with guests having to provide a password to enter your reception, and drinks served out of a big bathtub, as was the style during Prohibition. Your men can dress like gangsters and your ladies like flappers, and you can wear a big string of pearls to accent your era-appropriate dress.

COLOR-BASED

A black-and-white wedding might be your choice if you're more graphic in mindset. Imagine amazing white tablecloths with black runners, silver candelabras with white flowers, black charger plates under white china settings and a big black-and-white checkerboard dance floor. Guests can be asked to dress in black and white, and the only pop of color in the room is your lipstick-red bouquet. A bride's gotta stand out, right? If black-and-white is too stark for you, you might choose to base your personalized wedding on a different pair of colors, such as green and pink for a springtime look, or white and silver for a winter wedding. Each design decision grows out of this color scheme, slowly expanding to give you great options for a reception that looks like it's been designed by some of the top celebrity wedding luminaries in the business. What are some color scheme ideas that reflect your relationship?

The Number One Way to Have Your Wedding, Your Way

Why did I save it for now? If I had given you this step right off the bat, you might have skipped the other questions and exercises in this chapter. Those discussions were essential for you to be able to set the foundation on which your personalized plans must sit. A great wedding detail becomes greater when it fits perfectly into the larger picture of your wedding day. So there was a method here. And now you've arrived. What is the number one secret to planning your wedding your way? *Inserting your love story, your history as a couple, the entirely unique moments of your courtship and engagement into your wedding plans.*

Every personal moment between you, that first kiss, the first meal you cooked for him or he cooked for you, the first time he brought you Gerber daisies—it all becomes the one-of-a-kind DNA of your wedding day. No one else on Earth could ever have the same love story, and no one else can place each sentimental touchstone into your wedding like you can, as you turn your wedding day into a tribute to your love story. *That's* the best way to personalize your wedding day, breaking with tradition to make the day all about the two of you.

MINING THE PAST The weddings you've attended in the past can give you fabulous suggestions for what you do and don't want on your wedding day. Maybe you have attended a top-notch wedding that you wish to "borrow" from, or maybe you have attended a travesty of a wedding that had a band that took breaks every fifteen minutes and little more to eat than dry chicken. So take a few moments to mine the past for your leading recollections of past weddings and parties: *What worked at this wedding? What turned everyone off? What were people still raving about months later? Which elements of the weddings of close family and friends do you want to stay away from for fear of looking like you're copying them?*

So here we are at Phase Three, the pleasant and romantic task of thinking back over the shining moments of your courtship and engagement, looking for an overarching theme as well as the perfect creative touches for your ceremony and reception. Take notes here on the details of your big moments:

THE FIRST MEALS YOU COOKED FOR EACH OTHER

What was on the menu? Did you make your legendary lasagna, the lobster bisque you're known for, home-baked bread? Was it an authentic Italian meal, courtesy of your grandmother's recipes? Or a variety-is-the-spice-of-life tapas party that would be the perfect theme for your cocktail party? How did you set the table? Low white pillar candles that can be copied for the cocktail party tables? What was for dessert, and can that be added to your dessert menu?

YOUR FAVORITE FOODS

Over time, you've learned which meals you both love that you can have for your celebratory dinner, such as a filet mignon with garlic mashed potatoes and green beans with almond slivers. Whenever one of you has a triumph, that's on the menu. You know what the other loves on a pizza, so why not order up mini pizzas with mushroom or meatball, peppers or pineapple as passed hors d'oeuvres? He loves turkey burgers and you love feta-topped burgers, so mix them up as sliders offered at the cocktail party or as a snack for the after-party. For dessert, his love of cherry pie means multiple pies on the dessert table, while your favorite chocolate mousse served in martini glasses perfectly complements the cherry dessert.

YOUR FAVORITE WAYS TO ENJOY THE SEASON

For a fall wedding, you can incorporate the golds, burgundies, and persimmons of the autumn trees into your décor, or have a luscious soup bar with butternut squash soup at the cocktail party. For a winter wedding, your love of walking in the snow at night or decorating your house with strings of white lights could turn into great photo opportunities at a reception site you've chosen for its winter wonderland décor. Your love of summertime might place you at a beach locale with the ocean in the background and frozen drinks on your bar menu. In spring, it's all about the tulips and daffodils.

YOUR FIRST DANCE

What was the first song you ever slow-danced to? Is that the perfect song for your very first dance as husband and wife? Is there a beautiful love song your fiancé sent you or loaded into your iPod that would be your perfect First Dance song? Maybe you saw your favorite recording artist in concert at some point early in your dating days and always knew you wanted to dance to one of his songs at your wedding. Music is a top way to infuse both your ceremony and reception with a dose of *you* as a couple, so spend extra time on this one!

THE STORY OF YOUR ENGAGEMENT

If you got engaged on the beach at sunset—your groom did, after all, choose the perfect setting that would mean the most to you—your entire wedding could be based on the same romantic location and style. Was there champagne? Your favorite chocolate truffles? Was the engagement at a five-star restaurant where you enjoyed gourmet fare and white-glove service? Were you at a scenic overlook, enjoying the beauty of nature that you love so much? Your wedding, then, might be set out in nature, perhaps at that very same spot in the park. If you saw butterflies out in flower fields, there too are inspirations for your theme décor or your favors—you could place little sugar paste butterflies on boxes of chocolates and top your wedding cake with the same sugar paste butterflies. The smallest details from this momentous occasion can guide your artistic imagery for your wedding themes.

YOUR FAVORITE DRINKS

Build your bar menu with your favorite vintages of wine— perhaps the very same vintage you were drinking when you got engaged, or the wine you were drinking on your first date, or a bottle from the country of your heritage or one that matches your wedding's theme. Cocktails also work for this section of personalization ideas. Is there a particular kind of drink that you enjoyed on your first vacation together, perhaps a rum punch or a piña colada? Bring that into your day. Some couples have planned their color schemes around the hue of a cocktail enjoyed on their engagement weekend getaway.

YOUR FAVORITE POEM OR WRITINGS

If you or your groom regularly send poetry or romantic quotes to one another as a part of your love story, you can bring that touch of the classics into your invitations or wedding program, or place quote cards at each guest's seat. Lovers of Shakespeare have been inspired to plan their entire wedding around a *Midsummer Night's Dream* theme, bringing their wedding into the outdoors for a magical evening celebration with fairy lights in the trees and wandering musicians. All because they love the Bard, or regularly go to see Shakespearean plays as a shared passion. Literary weddings have encompassed Victorian themes, *Great Gatsby* themes, even Egyptian themes when the couple loves archaeology and the Egyptian culture, with hieroglyphics on their invitations and plenty of golds and jewel tones in their décor.

THE WAY YOU MET

Here are some ideas based on common "how I met" stories:

- **Did you meet at a football game as part of a group of friends who enjoyed a fun tailgate party then took in a championship game?** Your wedding, then, can reflect your shared love of the game, either in your team's colors or in the best tailgate casual reception anyone's ever been to, with gourmet grill stations outdoors.
- **Did you meet on a train as you commuted to work?** Twist that into an Orient Express–themed wedding.

- **Did you meet while overseas on vacation in Paris?** Design an Eiffel Tower wedding cake and set up your cocktail party to look like sidewalk bistros with red-and-white checked tablecloths. Your gown can be high fashion à la Paris's couture tone, as well.
- **Did you meet through an online dating service?** Make your wedding hi-tech, with guests RSVPing through your website and video monitors providing scenery on the walls. You might even print out your original online dating profiles to display on the family photos table to give everyone a look at what attracted you to one another.

THE THINGS YOU LOVE TO DO

If you're movie buffs, you might set your wedding up to resemble an Oscars awards celebration, complete with a red carpet outside, statuettes on each table, periodic "awards" presented throughout the night, and a copy of Wolfgang Puck's gourmet menu for the Governor's Ball, which you can find online at *www.oscars.org*. Or for a bit of fun and character you might arrange your wedding to reflect your favorite movie, such as *Casablanca, Gone with the Wind, The Wizard of Oz,* or every mob movie ever made. Your invitation might be made in the shape of a marquee, announcing your names as the stars of the show, and one of your food stations might offer movie-theater popcorn, nachos, candy, and other theater treats. For a Broadway-inspired wedding, your invitation might be designed in the form of a *Playbill* with your bridal party members' names listed as characters in your performance and the officiant listed as the director.

THE PLACES YOU LOVE TO GO

Vegas, baby! Or a beach theme, reflecting your love of the ocean, since you make an annual pilgrimage to the shore for your vacation. Some couples hold a destination wedding at the shore house, or in the shore town, where they have always vacationed, bringing extra sentimentality not just to their wedding day, but great memories set for every time they go back to their favorite getaway.

YOUR FAVORITE CAUSES

Since we are a society that's very focused on giving back to the world and protecting the environment, you might wish to design your wedding in a theme that pays homage to the cause in your heart.

A WORD OF WARNING Don't get too preachy about your pet cause, and don't choose a political party theme that can create tension (or screaming matches) in your crowd. You don't want to get too partisan and break up the party.

Here are some thought-provoking suggestions:

- You might choose an East-West theme and incorporate décor items and favors that have been made by fair-trade artisan co-ops who profit from your purchase.
- If you live an organic lifestyle, your menu may be organic, your tablecloths and napkins made of bamboo, and all of your menu items will be donated to a food pantry after the wedding.
- Since this is your day of love, you can share your passion with your guests as well as show off your conflict-free diamond ring and serve wines that return 20 percent of profit to a Third World community.
- In lieu of favors, make a donation to a cause. You might even choose a pink color theme to show your support for breast cancer research,

or go with red to pay homage to an AIDS charity or to the many groups helping to educate about heart health.

Think about the cause that unites you as a couple, and go from there.

Going for Graphics

You probably have several great ideas in mind now, so it's time to look for visuals to support your inspiration, or to show you that what seemed like a good idea at the time could actually backfire in a big way. This stage sends both of you to the computer so that you can look at the video samples on different videographers' websites. Do you like the group dance that's being shown? How about that romantic walk into the sunset? The candid footage of the bridal party dancing? And what's that behind the bridesmaids on the dance floor, waiting for the bouquet to be thrown? Are those bored wedding guests in the older generation back there, looking tired and waiting for the coffee to come out? The camera sees everything, so invest a few hours looking at this free-to-you wedding footage to gauge what different wedding elements *really* look like out there.

Believe it or not, YouTube is also a fun place to look, since every theme wedding possible is on there. If you're thinking about having your bridal party members learn a dance to perform with you, look first at some of the videos of groups putting on dance numbers—the good, the bad, and the tacky—to see if you really need that much going on at the start of your reception. See how your groom feels about doing a tango instead of a sway-side-to-side first dance. Done well, and with the right choreography, that could be far more *you* than a traditional dance, and here is where you find visual evidence to help you decide.

And finally, tear out selections of images from bridal magazines or print out images from websites to help you put pictures to the images in your minds. Your groom might surprise you by printing out the perfect graphic of a square wedding cake that fits his love of architecture. And you might find the perfect source for retro wedding invitations to suit your 1970s-theme wedding. The information is out there, and serendipity will often lead you right to the ideal photograph of the element you never knew you were looking for but is the perfect piece for your big day.

Do You Want a Destination Wedding?

It could be that getting out of town is all the *your way* you need.

I've mentioned destination weddings briefly here and there thus far, but now is when you explore whether or not a destination wedding is the answer to your wish for a unique, fun wedding done your way.

> **"** The only way we could limit our parents' guest lists, as well as our own with so many friends and colleagues in our lives, was to plan a destination wedding for just twenty guests. Our parents didn't want to obligate all of their friends and colleagues, and the relatives, to travel, so they dropped the enormous guest list topic. Planning a destination wedding allowed us to more easily plan out our wedding in our way, since it eliminated the biggest challenges we would have faced at home. **"** —*Patricia,* newlywed

The first issue to decide is whether or not you *both* want to take your wedding on the road, bringing just a handful of your nearest and dearest friends and relatives to a fabulous tropical resort or international city. This has to be a shared wedding dream, since the pros of a destination wedding can be offset by the drawbacks—namely, asking your guests to travel to a location of your choosing. With the expense of flying and lodging, do you really feel right essentially selecting where each family's annual vacation will be? Talk openly and honestly with each other about how your destination wedding wish and proposed locations would affect your parents, grandparents, siblings, and friends. Here are some factors to consider.

YOUR GUESTS' PHYSICAL ABILITY TO TRAVEL

For example, some couples would love to marry on St. John, but due to grandparents' ailing health and friends' pregnancies, would never pressure each other to take the wedding so far away. Yes, we're helping you have the wedding you want and not the one everyone else wants you to have, but there are limits to your personal preferences. "Getting your way" when you don't or won't think of others' life situations means you'll have empty chairs at your wedding. Sis won't be there, since her doctor won't allow her to fly during her third trimester. Grandma won't be there, since the trip would be just too much for her. Is it worth the risk?

THE COST TO YOUR GUESTS

Your next consideration is expense. And that depends heavily on the season of your wedding. With travel, a lot depends on peak-season and off-season, hurricane season and shoulder-season (the period of time just after peak-season and before off-season when prices drop 20 to 40 percent and the weather's just fine). Resorts may dip their prices in the fall months, since it's off-season for them, and skyrocket their prices in spring. It all depends on where they're located. And then there's airfare and lodging for three to five days, which is the average amount of time spent on location for a destination wedding.

LONG-DISTANCE PLANNING

A lot goes into planning a destination wedding. It may be long-distance planning, working with a resort's coordinator you've never met face-to-face. Or perhaps you may need to make an essential trip out there to meet with vendors and taste cakes. And then there's handling the complicated legalities of marriage licenses. Are you up for all of this, just to have a wedding that's different? Your answer may be a joyful *Yes!* As labor-intensive as a destination wedding can be, you might find it microscopic compared to the circus atmosphere, stress, stratospheric budget, and endless to-do list of a hometown wedding where your guest list would likely be far higher.

WHERE WILL YOU GO?

Next up: where do you want to go? Has it always been a dream of yours to visit Hawaii, and marrying there would be a fantasy beyond your dreams? Are you a subscriber to *Travel and Leisure*, practically drooling over their World's Best winners lists (*www.travelandleisure.com*) describing the many island and big-city resorts rated by jet-setters and travel connoisseurs as the height of luxury? Your wedding, then, may allow you to have your dream excursion your way, as well.

One growing trend is planning a destination wedding closer to home, such as at a beach or ski resort town just an hour away from home. Maybe you've vacationed there together, perhaps you got engaged there during your last visit, and no place on Earth could compare with the warm feelings you get when you go back each year. *That* is the only place for you.

CAN YOU CONTROL THE DETAILS?

When you plan a destination wedding, you're most often paired with a wedding coordinator or team of event experts, who in turn connect you with local vendors and other pros. This essential nature of planning from a distance means that you have to communicate well with all of these new-to-you experts, so that *they* can deliver your wedding, your way. This can be a challenge, since some resorts operate off of a "choose one item from this column, and one bouquet from these four pictures" system that is designed to make planning from a distance easier. You might appreciate the narrowed choices if that's your style. If not, find out first if you'll be able to supply graphics of cakes, flowers, décor and other wedding elements the way you want them. Some resorts will say, "No, we don't do anything outside of our existing portfolio." That is not the place for you, then. Be sure that you're not entranced by the beauty of a location to the point where you lose your planning freedom. Not all destination locations are built for custom planning, so research and interview well before you hand over deposits.

Now, with your decisions about destination weddings set, read on to find out how you can personalize your wedding exactly the way you want it . . . no matter where in the world you will be.

Your Compromise Worksheet

When you just can't agree on one style or one choice, it's time to compromise between your wishes. Use the following chart to keep track of who wants what, then jot down the compromise when you've reached one (you may find some options you both like in the next two chapters).

THE BRIDE WANTS	THE GROOM WANTS	THE COMPROMISE
_____	_____	_____
_____	_____	_____
_____	_____	_____
_____	_____	_____
_____	_____	_____
_____	_____	_____

CHAPTER 3

Tweaking the Traditional Ceremony Plans

The ceremony is the centerpiece of your wedding plans, the most important part of your day. It's where you join your lives together in the manner of *your* choosing, with the words and the music *you* want, the rituals that mean the most to *you*. Those parents who put pressure on brides and grooms to do what's "proper" or "expected," often laser-focus on the ceremony with strong-handed direction to follow religious protocol, to include the types of rituals that mean the most to *them*. Officiants, too, can weigh you down you with their lists of rules and regulations. They take marriage seriously, and they want to be sure you do too. Believing *their* way is the proper way, they might pressure you to include certain rites and wording, scripts and prompts, or to eliminate those elements they feel are too "out there" or inappropriate.

That's a lot of pressure for you to be under, especially if you and your fiancé disagree about the ideal way to compose and conduct your ceremony. One of you might love certain traditional elements such as lighting a unity candle, while the other suggests that unity *fireworks* would make far more of an impact.

This area of your wedding plans could feel like an intense tango, each of you moving forward, backward, and being plunged almost to the ground as you work to craft a ceremony that's *you*, reflecting *both* of your deepest beliefs and values. To help you start your process of designing your ideal personalized ceremony, let's look at how you might *twist* the age-old traditional ceremony elements. Why twist them? You might like the symbolism of wedding ceremony rituals, but you don't want to do them the way everyone else has done them. You don't want them prescribed to you. You want to be different, or have them reflect the true nature of your relationship. You don't want to eliminate them altogether, you just want to personalize them more.

> **"** I didn't want to be 'given away' when I walked down the aisle. I'm not a used car. So I thought a lot about how I could remove the 'giving the bride away' part of the processional while still honoring my father, and I came up with this: I had my Dad walk with me and kiss me at the end of the aisle, and then I walked forward toward my groom as he walked toward me. There was no placing of my hand on his to symbolize a transaction. There was no 'who gives this woman to this man' question. I pared away the distasteful parts, and still kept the moment special and meaningful. **"** — *Arielle*, **newlywed**

You get the picture. This is where you'll *tweak* the traditional ceremony elements to a far better plan for you. Throughout the rest of this chapter, I've listed the traditional Big Moments of a ceremony, and then provided you with some ways to modify them.

Religious Wedding Ceremonies

If you plan to marry in a house of worship, you might face a collection of rules and restrictions, since today's guiding forces at most houses of worship take their marriage rites very seriously. They may present you with a long list of what is and isn't permitted in their establishment, and some of these rules might strike you as questionable. No secular music? No photographs? You have to be a paying member for at least three years before the wedding? Granted, most are not as dramatic as these examples, but many couples say they were turned off by the harsh rules of a house of worship, which made their desires for *some* religious elements a bit trickier to incorporate into their ceremony, their way. Here is how you can marry in that house of worship but still tweak elements your way.

TRADITION   Getting Married in a Religious Location

Tweaks

- If your parents' church or synagogue has restrictive rules, look at a different house of worship, one that might be far more welcoming of personalized wedding ceremonies, nonmembers, and more secular elements. Shop around to find less strict houses of worship, and you may find your wedding's "home," a place that offers the propriety and tradition of a religious setting and the freedoms you need to plan your wedding your way. This other house of worship might be the same denomination as your parents' church, but it just feels better to you.

- If the sanctuary or cavernous church is way too grand and oppressive for you, ask if you can hold your ceremony on the house of worship's grounds, such as in their garden or in a smaller chapel.

- Find a house of worship that has great architecture, such as exposed ceiling beams and wide-open windows, fulfilling your need for a more modern setting as opposed to a closed-in, traditional setting with stained glass windows, heavy wooden pews, an enormous organ, a smaller layout, or other basic appearance issues.

- Ask if your religious officiant will perform your ceremony outside of the house of worship. In short, get out of the house, but take the religious leaders with you. Some will travel to your choice of setting in order to bless you with religious rites, while others say "No way."

- Look at nature as the ultimate religious location. Some couples say they feel closer to their chosen deities and spirituality when they're out in nature, so that's where they'd like to base their ceremony. With a natural setting, they can then infuse religious elements into the wording and rituals.

TRADITION Having a Religious Officiant

Tweaks

- If the leader at your particular house of worship is too strict, choose a religious officiant whom you have interviewed and found to be not quite as "old school" as yours. Many churches and synagogues have recently welcomed a more modern, younger set of officiants who may be a better personality fit with you. Don't be afraid to set up meetings with all of the officiants in that house of worship to interview additional possibilities.

- Choose a team of officiants, including one religious leader and one spiritual officiant not affiliated with a major denomination to reflect a better mix of your beliefs. Mixed-faith weddings are quite common, and many religious officiants will provide you with a list of their "tag team" partners in other houses of worship or spiritual associations.

- Check *www.celebrantusa.com* to find an independent minister or officiant to interview, seeing if this new person's style and experience meets your needs.

- Choose a secular officiant, such as a judge or mayor—whoever is sanctioned to perform weddings in your state or township—and then *you* infuse the religious elements into your personalized wedding by including psalms, scripture, religious music, and other important faith-based touches to your wedding.

- The same goes for having a friend or relative ordained to perform your ceremony, according to your state's rules on who can perform weddings. You can bring your chosen religious or spiritual elements into your own custom-written ceremony.

- Have your wedding rings blessed by a religious officiant before your wedding, even if a priest or rabbi will not perform the ceremony, so that you and your parents know that you brought in a blessing that suits your needs.

TRADITION Using the Church or Synagogue's Musicians

Tweaks

- Before you dismiss the idea based on your earlier-in-life experiences of somber singing or funereal organ music, check out the new, modern performances that the house of worship may feature. Styles may have changed since your early religious exposure, and that house of worship might feature an awesome singing group or musician.

- Ask about the different types of choirs the site offers, such as a gospel group, a children's choir, an a cappella group, guitarists rather than organists, and other unique musical acts.

- Say "No" to any stale or stodgy musical acts the church offers. Rather than fear hurting the kindly pianist's feelings, just let them know you have a different plan in mind by offering specific suggestions, perhaps with sheet music found online, that better suit your plans.

- Bring in your own musicians, such as the pianist you discovered at a hotel brunch, a singer you found at a coffee shop, or a music student from a nearby university. Get permission before you book, though. Some sites really will not let you bring in outside performers.

- Ask if you can have a talented friend or family member step in to perform the music for your ceremony.

- Skip the musical interludes and just arrange for pre-wedding, processional, and recessional music if you have always disliked how extra musical numbers placed in the middle of ceremonies stretched out the length of the event.

PAY TO PLAY   If the house of worship requires a small donation in order to allow you to bring in your own hired musicians, just pay it. You may find it worth the $20 to get the musical performance you desire.

- If the site is wired for sound, ask if you can play your choice of prerecorded classical or site-appropriate songs. And keep in mind that some officiants will want to approve your song list first. It's just part of the deal.

TRADITION: Adhering to the Church or Synagogue's "Script"

Tweaks

- Rather than surrender to the house of worship's script for what the officiant will say, how you will respond, approved readings, etc.—which often were put together years ago to streamline wedding ceremonies—ask if you can be granted creative control to adjust the wording that you will use. Many officiants will grant you the power of the red pen to cross out phrases that don't sit right with you, and some will even sit down to work with you on a script that fulfills both of your requirements.

- You have to speak up if you want to eliminate a mass or offerings. Be respectfully assertive, and ask to cross off the parts of the ceremony that are too heavy-handed or that stretch the ceremony out too long.

REPLACE THIS . . .   *With this ring, I pledge thee my troth.*

With this . . .

With this ring, I promise my life, love, and fidelity to you.

Few religious officiants will have a problem with ditching the antiquated language. They too might not even know what a "troth" is.

- If certain scriptures are suggested to you, ask if you can replace them with your choices, or with your own personally worded readings.

- Ask to change the order of ceremony elements, such as lighting the unity candle after you exchange rings.

- If the officiant is not okay with your wishes to change the script, walk away and find a site and religious leader who understands that this is your ceremony and that you feel strongly about combining your religious values with your more personal ceremony elements.

TRADITION: Presentation of Religious Offerings

Tweaks

- Presenting the wine or the host for mass is an honored position, so treat it as such. But rather than have church elders perform the rite as some churches require, ask to have parents or honored guests step in instead.

- Include family heirlooms like platters or wine goblets that were used at your parents' and grandparents' wedding ceremonies in these religious rites.

TRADITION: Holding a Mass

Tweaks

- If you will include a full mass in your ceremony, you can shorten the duration of this ritual by having three people present the host and wine to your guests, with three lines formed at the front of the church rather than only one. Again, see if any wedding guests are qualified to help distribute the host and wine.

- Skip the mass, which many of your guests will not mind. Some couples plan to attend a full mass, together with their parents, on the day after the wedding to fulfill their wishes for a mass attendance in that calendar week. You may be able to make this part of your wedding weekend, not your ceremony per se. The hotel may even have a free shuttle bus available to take guests to the church the next day.

Both Religious and Nonreligious Wedding Ceremonies

TRADITION: Not Seeing Each Other Before the Wedding

Tweaks

- Ditch it altogether! Meet up before the ceremony to *really* get the effect of your groom seeing you for the first time in your gown. Then you'll be able to talk to each other, and you'll look perfect for pre-wedding photos. This plan also saves time immediately after the ceremony, delivering you right to your cocktail party since you don't have to pose for a half hour of pictures together right after the ceremony.

- In some religions, this is when you'll sign your marriage contract, so it's a good time to fulfill valued traditions.

- Plan to see each other from a distance in a romantic new practice where you're up on a balcony and your groom is below, admiring you. If you'd like, you can then walk with each other down the aisle to be married.

TRADITION: Isolating the Groom Before the Ceremony

Tweaks

- The groom can emerge from his isolation to greet guests at the door and escort relatives and friends to their seats if he wishes.

- The groom might wish to escort his parents to their seats as part of the preprocessional.

- If the ceremony takes place at a nonreligious site where champagne is served to arriving guests, he could enjoy a drink with the guests.

TRADITION: Distributing Folded Programs

Tweaks

- Go "green" and save paper. Print your own programs on single-panel cards, printed two to a page on thicker card stock, featuring just the names of the bridal party, parents, and officiant. Guests don't need a play-by-play of what's happening in the ceremony.

- Get creative. Print your program details on paper fans that guests can use to cool themselves during summer and outdoor weddings.

- Change the shape of programs. Print out your chosen wording onto thicker cardstock, and then cut each one into a circle or heart shape to match your theme décor.

- Create scrolls with program information on them. Roll each page and tie with a simple, color-coordinated ribbon.

- Ask the child attendants to stand at the ceremony entrance handing out programs to each guest.

- Some parents now want to be the first to greet arriving guests, so ask them to hand out programs at the entrance to the ceremony.

- If you chose to have a smaller bridal party, or no bridal party at all, your most-honored friends or siblings can instead be in charge of greeting guests and handing out programs at the ceremony entrance.

- If you've hired performers for your theme wedding—such as Irish step, salsa, flamenco, or ballet dancers in costume—ask several of them to stand at the ceremony entrance to hand out programs to your guests, who get a great preview of the fun and interactive wedding ahead of them. You might also have musicians at the ceremony entrance playing theme-setting music as guests arrive.

• Not into the work and expense of printed programs? Skip the printed programs and have all major participants' names listed on the backs of the menu cards on guests' tables at the reception, with a note thanking them and guests for participating in the wedding.

• Again, you can skip the printed programs and have a sign at the entrance to the ceremony site. It could feature an enlarged photo of the two of you and, beneath that, a listing of the names of the parents, bridal party members, officiants, and participants written in an elegant font. At theme weddings, bridal party members might get nicknames on this sign, such as Greg "The Lifeguard" Smith and Belinda "The Beach Bunny" Jones at your beach-themed wedding, or Michael "The Maestro" Anderson at your opera-themed wedding.

TRADITION: Having Groomsmen Seat the Guests

Tweaks

• Older ring bearers can also seat guests in a charming twist on tradition, either joining the groomsmen in doing so or as the only greeters and seaters.

• Bridesmaids can reveal themselves early to mingle, greet, and help escort guests to their seats. Why should the men have all the fun?

• Guests can escort themselves to their seats, leaving the men free of an extra duty.

TRADITION: Having a Bride's Side and a Groom's Side for Guests' Seating

Tweaks

• Mix up the guests so that there's *no* bride's side and groom's side

• Seat people as they arrive so that all of the front rows are filled nicely and so that there's no huge discrepancy between your packed side of the aisle and your groom's sparse number of guests (or vice versa).

• If your site has two aisles and three seating sections, or if you can arrange that layout through your chair placement scheme, that allows for peaceful seating when there are divorced parents. You can then have a section for your parents, a section for the groom's mother and her new husband and their guests, and a section for the groom's father and his girlfriend and their guests. For guest mingling, one of those three sections can be reserved for all of your friends.

TRADITION: Traditional or Classic Pre-Ceremony Music

Tweaks

• Choose songs from your love story, and provide the stories behind each song—such as "We danced our first slow dance ever to this song"—in your printed wedding programs.

• Have live musicians playing unique instruments, such as Asian flute or drums, sitar, or other performance treats.

• Choose songs that work with the theme of your wedding, such as 1940s music for your USO-themed party or big-screen soundtrack songs for your movie-lover's wedding.

TRADITION: Escorting Mothers to Their Seats

Tweaks

- If you have stepmothers, they too may be given a special place in the preprocessional seating lineup, preceding the mothers.

- Grandmothers and godmothers may also be seated specially.

- Choose a song for the seating of the mothers—in fact, *they* may join together to select their one seating song—to set them apart and allow them to personalize their big moment.

- Mothers, including the mother of the groom, may be escorted by their sons, by a spouse, or—as in the case of a widow—by another honored male guest, such as the departed husband's brother. Grandchildren may also escort these honored women to their seats.

- If you'll have both your parents escort you down the aisle, this portion of the preprocessional may be skipped.

TRADITION: Having Bridesmaids Walk in the Processional

Tweaks

- If you find it too old-fashioned or expected to have bridesmaids walk down the aisle alone, allow the groomsmen to escort the ladies down the aisle for great photo opportunities and a classy look. Child attendants may also walk down the aisle with the bridesmaids.

- If you have a large number of bridesmaids, allow them to walk down the aisle in pairs, while the maid or matron of honor is the only one to walk unescorted so she is set apart as an honored member of the bridal party.

TRADITION: Having Your Father Escort You Down the Aisle

Tweaks:

- Your biological dad can walk you halfway down the aisle, then hand you off to your awaiting stepdad, who will then bring you to your groom, or vice versa.

- You can have both your dad and your mom escort you down the aisle.

- If your father has passed away, you might ask your brother, or your father's brother, or your grandfather to do the honors.

- If your mom has been your sole parent, she can walk you down the aisle.

- You can ask your siblings to escort you.

- Your groom may walk with you.

- If you have kids, they can be the ones to escort you down the aisle.

- Or, you can walk unaccompanied, eschewing the concept of being "given away" to your groom. You've walked proudly and confidently through life, and now you'll do the same as you approach your marriage.

TRADITION: Playing Traditional Processional Music

Tweaks

- Again, bring in that secular, modern music you love.

- Play songs from your love story.

- Surprise your groom by choosing a meaningful song that is both your processional walk music *and* a dedication to him.

- Invite your kids to help you choose your processional music.

- Walk to the sounds of your live musicians.

- If you're by the ocean, just have the sounds of the surf be your background "music."

- Choose a more upbeat, unexpected, or quirky song, rather than a classical song that everyone expects.

- Choose an additional "Your Song" to walk down the aisle to.

TRADITION: Having Traditional Ceremony Readings

Tweaks

- Instead of having two or three traditional readings, including scripture or poetry, choose *one* to suit your need for tradition, and then add several more contemporary choices.

- Write your own readings, such as essays or poetry you both have written about the depth of your relationship and the meaning of marriage.

- If a relative or friend has written an inspiring and beautiful poem or essay, include that in your ceremony.

- Invite a writer friend to create and deliver an inspiring reading as his or her ceremony gift to you.

- Take a traditional reading and *add* to it, such as expanding on its meaning to you.

TRADITION: Performing Traditional Wedding Vows

Tweaks

- The tried-and-true litany of *to have and to hold* is, to some, the quintessential collection of marital promises. They build their modernized, personalized weddings *around* traditional vows—and you might, too, if that's your wish. If you'd like to tweak them, though, add a few extra lines on the end, such as "in trials and in challenges, in all seasons, when you're feeling strong, when you need a boost," and so on. There are so many dualities to play with, so sit down and brainstorm your versions of "in sickness and in health, in good times and in bad."

- Build your vows off of a poem, song lyrics, or a quote such as Ovid's "If thou wouldst marry wisely, marry thy equal." Your vows, then, can expound upon how you establish and honor your equality in marriage.

- Allow some humor into your vows, with statements that are very *you*, such as promising to indulge the other's passion to travel the world, as long as the destination does not require vaccinations (you can recall a trip you took which required painful shots first).

- Include your children in your vows, if you're blending families.

- Surprise each other with vows you've written in secret, revealing them only now in front of your loved ones.

- Combine your vows and the exchange of rings, speaking your promises right before you slip that ring on your partner's finger.

- Exchange your vows in your languages of origin.

TRADITION: Exchanging Your Rings

Tweaks

- Have your rings blessed by a religious officiant before the wedding, so that you know they're infused with the faith element you might not have included in your ceremony.

- Have a reading performed about the symbolism of the rings.

- Share the story of what your ring choices mean to you, such as an entwined design symbolizing the closeness you'll always share.

- Share what you've had inscribed inside your rings, which may also be a surprise you've planned for one another.

- If you're exchanging heirloom rings from relatives who were married for fifty years, share that story with your guests.

TRADITION: Lighting a Unity Candle

Tweaks

- Instead of the traditional two taper candles on the sides of one thicker single-wick candle, use a wider three-wick pillar candle to symbolize your past, present, and future, or faith, hope, and love.

- Each of you pour a cup of same-colored sand into a larger glass vase so that there is no evidence of whose sand is whose . . . it's all just yours.

- Design a unique style of unity candle, such as a square or oval, or a unique color beyond white, such as one that matches the décor of your home.

- Incorporate a love of all things organic by using a soy candle.

- Make your own unity candle using materials found in the craft store, and embed pearls or gemstones in your choice of design.

- Have grandparents and parents light their own tapers and place them by your unity candle.

- Instead of a unity candle, make it a planting by pressing seeds or bulbs into a soil-ready flowerpot to symbolize the new life you're planting together.

- Use wine as a unity ritual. Each of you pours a small glass of wine into a larger glass, and then you both drink from it.

TRADITION: Enacting a Cultural-Unity Ritual

Tweaks

- Bind your hands with a braided cord as a blessing is said over you in a traditional handfast ritual.

- Have your officiant drape your shoulders with a cultural shawl to symbolize your shared protection in life.

- Walk together in a circle around the altar to symbolize the first steps you're taking as husband and wife.

- Exchange symbolic food items such as figs or bread, whatever is used in your cultural marriage rites.

- Each of you takes a bite of a sweet item, such as a petit four or strawberry, to bring sweetness to your marriage.

- Have your parents present you with symbolic food or drink items from your heritage's marriage rites.

TRADITION: Sealing Your Vows with a Kiss

Tweaks

- This one you might not want to tweak too much, but you can add a chivalrous kiss of your hand after the kiss on the lips.

- Pay homage to your European backgrounds with a secondary exchange of kisses on both cheeks.

- Kiss your fingertips and then place them on your partner's wrist so that the pulse carries it straight to his or her heart.

TRADITION: Being Presented to Your Guests as Husband and Wife

Tweaks

- Use both names if you're hyphenating, such as *Mr. Anthony Smith and Mrs. Anne Jones-Smith.*

- Ask an honored relative or friend to be the one to announce you for the first time as husband and wife.

- Announce yourselves as husband and wife, by saying, "I'd like to present my wife, (name)" and "I'd like to present my husband, (name)."

- Your children can be the ones to announce you as husband and wife.

- Your parents can be the ones to announce you as husband and wife.

TRADITION: Walking in the Recessional

Tweaks

- You can just have the bridesmaids follow you while the groomsmen stay behind to "release" rows of guests.

- Your parents could follow you down the aisle, so that they can be the first ones to hug and greet you.

- Your children can be sent down the aisle to greet you first.

- Play upbeat music so that participants can dance their way back up the aisle.

- Instruct guests to blow bubbles at you as you enact the recessional, rather than having the bubbles used for your getaway car dash. Just make sure your location approves the use of bubbles. Some have sworn off this tradition due to slippery flooring afterwards.

TRADITION: Enacting a Receiving Line

Tweaks

- Scrap the receiving line so that you can slip away to get started on those post-ceremony photos. Instead, visit with guests at their tables in the reception hall and get far better mingling time with them.

- Shorten the receiving line by just having it consist of the two of you and your parents, plus your Maid of Honor and Best Man. This makes a much faster process than if you included all of the bridesmaids and groomsmen, as has been a traditional option in the past.

- As guests pass through the receiving line, you hand them single-stem flowers as their in-the-moment favors and an immediate thank-you for sharing your big moment.

- Choose a lovely setting for the receiving line, such as under a tree or on a nearby terrace, not on the stairs outside the church. This idea helps you move to perhaps a shadier location if it's hot out, and avoid a traffic jam at the doors of the church as guests wait to see you.

- Sprinkle rose petals along the path of the receiving line, or create a colorful aisle runner for this purpose.

- Hold your receiving line at the entrance to the cocktail party.

TRADITION: Signing the Marriage License or Ketubah

Tweaks

- Make sure you're present when it's signed so that you don't miss the big moment.

- Use a special, ceremonial pen that you will keep after the wedding.

- Ask the couple who introduced you to be your license witnesses.

- At that moment, present your officiant and witnesses with thank-you gifts.

- Take photos of the license or ketubah being signed.

TRADITION: Posing for Post-Ceremony Photos

Tweaks

- Some photographers will instruct you to go back inside the house of worship, or your ceremony site, to stage the big moments of your ceremony for extra photos to be taken. If this doesn't feel right to you, just decline. You may have limited time before your cocktail party, and with so many extra shots to get, this indulgence may not be necessary (unless the pro says he missed a vital picture).

- Arrange to have full group photos, including all guests, taken right outside the ceremony site to save time.

- Limit your photographer to a set amount of time for post-ceremony photos so that you have plenty of time to enjoy your cocktail party.

- Skip the posed, lineup shots with your bridal party if those are not your style, and instead, ask your photographer to snap candid shots of all of you interacting after the ceremony.

- Arrange to have additional bridal party and family photos taken at the end of the cocktail party before you're introduced into the room at the reception. This fifteen minutes between events may be the perfect time to take those group shots.

- Since many brides and grooms want their guests to get dress-up family portraits at the wedding, have your emcee make an announcement that the photographer will be set up in the garden for anyone wishing to have their own photos taken. These shots become terrific gifts for guest couples and families later.

TRADITION: Dashing to Your Awaiting Getaway Car

Tweaks

- If your ceremony and reception are in one place, you won't need to enact this tradition.

- Most sites forbid birdseed and rice tosses as you run to the car, so provide guests with bubble bottles or bells instead.

- If you don't want to be showered with anything, instruct your bridal party to begin a round of applause or a great chant as you dash to your car.

- Inside the car, share a champagne toast and some snacks from a prepacked picnic basket, since you may not have had much of an appetite before the wedding. Some gourmet treats will hit the spot and energize you for the photo-taking session to follow.

- Your private moments inside the car are also the perfect time to exchange cards or gifts, or share your first impressions of the ceremony, tell your spouse how much you loved seeing him/her for the first time, and get some privacy for a terrific, passionate kiss.

CHAPTER 4

Tweaking the Traditional Reception Plans

Now that you've tweaked your ceremony plans, finding the right balance between tradition and personalized-yet-proper elements, it's now time to look at your reception with the same goal. How are you going to plan your reception, your way? Use this list of traditional reception elements, the so-called Big Moments, as your guide, and consider the suggested tweaks as your plan or as springboards to your own, custom ideas:

TRADITION: Having a Separate Cocktail Party

Tweaks

- In the past, the bride, groom, and bridal party were ushered to a private room, separate from where the cocktail party is underway, where they would enjoy their own private drinks and cocktail party fare. While the concept is understandable—allowing you time to eat and drink before guests mob you—you might not want to miss out on being mobbed by your friends and family. That closed-door party might not be your style, so skip it and join the party.

- Allow yourselves twenty minutes of this private party so that you can get a few bites to eat and enjoy a toast with your bridal party, and then go join the ongoing cocktail party in the next room.

- Grab a private snack fest just for the two of you, before you head out into the party after twenty or so minutes of alone time.

TRADITION: Being Introduced into the Room

Tweaks

- Since parents are usually introduced formally into the room as the start of the grand entrances, choose a theme song for the parents' introduction and entrance.

- If parents are unmarried, allow them to choose their escorts. It may be a grandchild or the flower girls and ring bearers holding their grand-parents' hands.

- Bridal party members may be introduced into the room in pairs or trios, whatever makes the most sense for your grouping of men and women.

- For your entrance into the room, you might wish to make a dramatic, celebrity-worthy wardrobe change into a different party gown, even with your hair in a different style.

- Choose a terrific theme song for *your* introduction into the room.

- Ask the emcee to read your creative one-liners in introducing all the members of your bridal party, such as sharing who each person is (e.g., "sister of the bride") and a fun factoid about each one (e.g., "she introduced the bride and groom" or "he drove the groom over here to seal his fate.")

- For your introduction, the emcee might announce that you have now been married for twenty-eight minutes.

- For a fun and funny entrance, ask your emcee to imitate that famous announcer who shouts, "Let's get ready to rumble!"

- Ask a friend or relative to act as emcee, sharing those great one-liners as surprises to the two of you.

- Have your children introduced right before you, as honored guests.

- If you're not the spotlight types, or if one or both of you is shy, you can opt to eliminate the announcing-in ritual and just enter the room together with your guests and without fanfare. This could eliminate the ten-minute introductions of everyone in your bridal party, who then line up awkwardly on the dance floor to watch your first dance. You might wish for everyone to just sit down naturally.

TRADITION: Sharing Your First Dance

Tweaks

- Rather than sway side to side through a long, sentimental slow song, *start off* with the romantic song everyone expects and then transition into a faster song, a tango, or other unique dance.

- Choreograph a superb partnership dance number, either through your own making or with the help of a professional dance instructor.

- To add a bit of humor, if that's your style, start off dancing incredibly badly (guests' jaws will drop at your lack of rhythm), and then make a show of starting over and performing that expertly choreographed and well-rehearsed dance number à la Fred Astaire and Ginger Rogers.

- For a theme wedding, add props to your dance number, such as a top hat and cane for your groom, a feather boa for you, or other options. Think twice about ripping your skirt off to reveal a sparkly, sequined dress, as you may have seen on some of those "what were they thinking?" wedding video programs on TV or YouTube, since that can be a little much for this big moment. Unless your personal style is "a little much," and that strip-down is perfectly in keeping with your dramatic taste.

- Enlist your bridal party as your backup dancers, giving them easy steps and hand motions to go along with the music. It's a fun backdrop to your spotlight dance.

- Invite your children to join you on the dance floor as you each dance with the kids, or dance as a group.

- If either of you are shy about dancing in front of a crowd with all eyes on you, ask the emcee to give you just a few minutes of a couple dance and then invite all of the guests to join you on the dance floor.

TRADITION: The Father-Daughter Dance

Tweaks

- Start with a slow, sentimental song, and then switch into a fun, upbeat song that might reflect your fun-loving relationship far better.

- If you have both a father and stepfather, plan to dance half a song with one and then dance with the other.

- If your father is departed, share this dance with his brother, or with *your* brother, as an honored fill-in.

- Props and wardrobe changes are perfect for the dads as well, so a fun jacket, top hat and cane may be ideal for his theatrical side. He may love breaking with tradition as well.

- As you dance, have a video screen behind you, on which you'll display old home video of you as a little girl, dancing on top of your dad's shoes. There won't be a dry eye in the house.

- Skip this dance if you're not close with your father. It's your wedding, your way. You don't have to dance with the guy if he's never been nice to you.

TRADITION: The Mother-Son Dance

Tweaks

- Choose a sentimental song, and then switch into a faster, perhaps even funny, song for your dance.

- Invest the time to choreograph your dance number together so that she knows when you're going to twirl her and so that the number impresses the guests and gives you both confidence in what could otherwise be an awkward dance.

- Play childhood video of the two of you in the background as you dance.

- If your mother is departed, share this dance with her sister, or with your sister, as an honored fill-in.

- Skip this dance if you're not close with your mother. Why put on an act of being close when you're not?

TRADITION: The Best Man's Toast

Tweaks

- Keep the toast short and sweet, as opposed to a long, rambling toast.

- Include snippets of marriage wisdom that he's collected from wedding guests, thereby including *them* in his spotlight moment as well.

- The best man can be joined by the groomsmen in a toast sent from all of them.

- The best man can introduce a short video toast that he has filmed and edited, including funny scenes and stories. This option works wonderfully for a best man who fears public speaking.

TRADITION: Requesting Blocks of Song Types

Tweaks

- Play slow songs, perfect for slow dancing, during the entire dinner.

- Play faster music from the older generation's era, so that they can shake it on the dance floor to music with which they are familiar.

- Create music theme blocks, such as four or five Latin songs followed by four or five Motown songs, keeping guests on the dance floor for a succession of songs in their own favorite stylings.

- If line dances are not your style, tell the band or deejay they're on the Don't Play list.

- If you want, ban all cliché music, including the songs you hear at every other wedding.

- Keep control of your song list by telling the band or deejay to clear all song requests through you first.

- Consider skipping certain types of hip-hop or club music that you and your friends can enjoy after the wedding at a nightclub. Your mixed crowd will appreciate being spared distasteful lyrics and such.

- End the night with a fresh block of slow dance songs, to cap off your wedding experience with romance.

TRADITION: Cutting the Cake

Tweaks

- Skip the tradition of smashing cake into each other's faces. That's so 1983. Instead, display trust by feeding each other neatly.

- You can dot each other's noses with a fingertip of frosting.

- Use heirloom cake knives, perhaps the ones your parents or grandparents used at their weddings, and share that story with your guests.

- If you have children at the wedding, make it a group cake feeding, with them getting to dot your nose with frosting as well.

TRADITION: The Maid of Honor's Toast

Tweaks

Use any of the ideas from the best man's toast tweaks above.

- As a tweak for both her and the best man's toast, the microphone can be handed off to the people who introduced the two of you, allowing them to say a few words as well.

TRADITION: Tossing the Bouquet

Tweaks

- Fewer brides are tossing the bouquet to their screaming, drunk, single women friends. Instead, present your bouquet to your mother, grandmother, a favorite aunt, or your daughter.

- Present your bouquet to the longest-married couple in the room.

- Present your bouquet to your officiant as a meaningful take-home thank you for joining you in marriage.

- Bring a smaller version of your bouquet to the reception, and toss that to your awaiting women. And if you have only a few single women in your crowd, invite *all* of your female guests onto the dance floor to catch your bouquet that now symbolizes many years of happiness, rather than its old incarnation as a symbol of being the next to marry.

TRADITION: Tossing the Garter

Tweaks

- Many couples are choosing to skip the garter toss, as it is déclassé to remove it from the bride's thigh while in front of mixed company, including children.

- Replace the garter with an ankle bracelet that the groom may remove from the bride's ankle, place in a fabric pouch, and throw to male guests for placement on the bouquet-catcher's ankle.

- As a twist on the above idea, that man can be invited to present the ankle bracelet to his own date or spouse.

TRADITION: The Last Dance

Tweaks

- Choose a slow, romantic song with terrific lyrics for you both to dance to as the last song of the evening.

- Choose a song that has romantic significance in your love story, such as the first song you ever slow-danced to when you were first dating, and share that story with your guests.

- Turn this last dance into your departure, as you dance your way out the door, waving to your guests.

- If both of you have had too much to drink, skip this spotlight dance because it's not going to be pretty to see you stumbling or having you dropped during a dip, or fall during a twirl.

TRADITION: Your Departure

Tweaks

- Take the microphone to thank your guests for coming to the wedding.

- Take this time to dash to your awaiting car, with guests invited outside to wave good-bye to you. Stop to hug your parents good-bye, which makes for unforgettable memories and great pictures.

- Surprise your partner with a dramatic exit, such as by yacht, classic car, exotic rented car, horse and carriage, helicopter, or decorated car. Also great memories and pictures.

Keep, Eliminate, or Tweak

Now that you've looked through some options for customizing your wedding ceremony and reception, record the traditional wedding elements you'd like to keep as is, remove from your wedding plans, or tweak to a form that works better for you . . .

ELIMINATE

- _____
  _____
- _____
  _____
- _____
  _____

TWEAK

- _____
  _____
- _____
  _____
- _____
  _____

Part Two

SHARING YOUR PLANS WITH OTHERS

Okay, now you're ready to—cue scary music here—break the news about your special plans to your parents and grandparents, who have wishes and demands of their own for your big day. How do you let them know that you have specific wants and needs, likes and dislikes, for your big day, and that the wedding you have in mind could surprise (if not stun) them? Read on for a complete primer on taking these first, essential, basic steps in planning your wedding, your way.

CHAPTER 5

Breaking the News to Parents and Grandparents

You don't *need* your parents' approval to design your own wedding day, but it can make the entire process much more peaceful if they understand what you plan to do—especially if they're paying for all or part of the wedding. Some parents and grandparents have strong opinions about "how things are done" and "what will people think?" The average bride and groom want peace and harmony on their planning team as they enjoy putting their big day together, so this chapter offers diplomacy scripts on how to share your unique plans. Here is what *not* to say, what *not* to do, and how to reach a state of peace and cooperation for the rest of your planning season.

Understanding Where They're Coming From

The key to approaching your parents, grandparents, and yes, your in-laws is good diplomacy, and the key to good diplomacy is understanding what's behind their mindset. You're going to have far more success in your talks with elders if you can address their values and concerns, rather than just walking up to them and saying, "It's my way or the highway." Being aggressive and bossy—and insensitive—isn't going to get you anywhere good, and pretty soon you'll wind up like one of those drama-soaked couples whose parents refuse to come to the wedding.

No matter how involved your parents will be with planning and paying for the wedding, you can prevent hurt feelings as you partner with them. Since every parent is different, with his or her own particular expectations for the wedding *and* his or her own partnering abilities, I can't just script your approach in a one-size-fits-all way. You'll have to do some homework before your conversation.

The first step is understanding where your parents, grandparents, and future in-laws stand when it comes to today's modern wedding. Some parents have heard enough of their friends' stories about planning their kids' weddings that they know tradition can sometimes fly out the window. They might be very well-adjusted parents who have never had a problem granting your wishes. If this is the case, skip right into the next planning chapter. If this is *not* the case, and if your parents are likely to have some trouble adjusting to your dream wedding plans—as most couples experience these days—get ready to make life way easier on yourselves.

Where do your parents, grandparents, and future in-laws fit on this scale?

- Unconditional love for you, wanting your wedding vision exactly the way you want it . . . OR
- Will go along with what you want, but may throw a major guilt trip or two
- Laser-focused on how they want the wedding to be, self-centered, don't realize (or care) that they're being selfish?

Realize That You Can't Change Them

Regardless of the mindset of your parents, grandparents, or in-laws, here's one important fact to know: *you can't change their personalities.* If a parent has always been greedy and controlling, that's how he or she is going to be with the wedding plans. It may sound simple, but you'd be surprised at how many couples get hurt and frustrated because they believed their parents would magically turn into genies who grant every wish with a smile. You have to accept reality. Some parents, grandparents, and future in-laws are going to be difficult. They want you to have the wedding the way they want it to be, and they're going to pull out every weapon in their arsenal to make it that way.

> **"**I have pictures of myself as a little girl, probably three years old, when my mother dressed me up as a bride for every Halloween until I could pick my own costumes. it seems like she's been planning my wedding day since before I was born. So it terrified me to tell her that she's not getting her wedding dream through me.**"** —*Eliza*, **bride-to-be**

Deal with Your Own Fears

As you think about telling your family about your special wedding plans, you're probably facing three main fears about your parents, grandparents, or in-laws:

1. They will pull their financial help away.
2. You'll disappoint them.
3. You're dreading a confrontation with them.

Eliza says her heart was pounding and she was sweating when she drove over to her mother's house to tell her about her plans for a nontraditional wedding, worried that her mom would start to cry. Grooms, too, say they worry about confrontations with their parents, since they don't want their parents to dislike their brides for wrecking their own long-held wedding visions. There are a lot of sweaty palms out there.

Now, let's look at what actual parents say their fears are:

- **"I don't want the rest of the family to think my daughter is immature, or not taking marriage seriously."** *Ouch. That's "what will people think?" mixed in with "you're not what you should be"—the toxic cocktail of parental disapproval.*
- **"I don't want this wedding to be the only wacky wedding in the family when we've always had religious, formal weddings. The couple will surely regret this plan later."** *You're breaking with tradition in your own lineage now, and some parents take this as an insult to how they and every other ancestor chose to get married. Plus a dose of "what will people think?"*
- **"I can't accept that their marriage will not be recognized by the church."** *Parents, grandparents, and in-laws may take their religious rules very seriously, and so they may push to have your marriage sanctioned by their house of worship. Some parents say that future grandchildren would not be allowed to be baptized in the church if this marriage is not recognized by the church. They're looking way ahead at a future catastrophe. You're condemning your unborn children's souls, they think, so that's why they're pushing for the church wedding.*
- **"I worry that not having wedding traditions will bring bad luck to the couple."** *Your superstitious mom who throws salt over her shoulder and feng shuis the house has tapped into that fear of evil spirits. Deep*

down, this may be the least troubling mindset, since it's almost entirely comprised of concern for your well-being and happiness. There's no "what will people think" involved here.

- **"If they have this theme wedding, it's going to look ridiculous when it happens during the same summer as my brother's daughter's formal wedding!"** *Say it with me, now. . . . What are people going to think?*

- **"Now I'll never get to plan the wedding *I* wanted when I got married, that my parents stepped in and planned because they were paying for it."** *Okay, so no actual parent is going to say that out loud, but chances are pretty good that there is at least some of this in a difficult parent's bag full of issues. You've just destroyed their chance to plan their wedding, their way. How could you!?*

What *Not* to Do

You can learn the most from others' mistakes, so I've compiled a bunch for you to review. These are mistakes other couples have made that you should avoid at all cost:

DON'T send an e-mail telling parents you already have everything planned, but you'll come over to talk with them about x, y, and z, which are still open for discussion. Trying to pre-empt through the protective cloak of e-mail makes you look cowardly and parents feel blindsided.

DON'T just drop in with your announcement and expect them to drop everything to talk about your wedding. Always make advance plans to get together for dinner or a visit.

DON'T avoid the topic for weeks, figuring that it would make sense to them that you've already booked your experts. Stalling is not a good idea.

DON'T have this conversation when both sets of parents are meeting each other for the first time. It's way too emotionally loaded. Just tell them the planning comes later; now is getting-to-know-you time.

DON'T accept their money while being vague about the plans. This one is a big one, since parents often happily hand over the check with expectations that they'll be fully involved in the wedding plans. And they may already have certain expectations for the wedding—especially if you've had past conversations about what style of wedding you are envisioning . . . but those are no longer your current plans.

PAST CONVERSATIONS Can you blame parents for thinking you are going to have a formal, big wedding when you *said* that's what you were going to do? Granted, you might have said that five years ago, before you met your fiancé, but parents remember. And some parents fear that you want a unique wedding now because that's what your groom wants. They're just being protective, so be sure to say, "I know I said in the past that I wanted a big, traditional wedding, but I'm feeling more excited about a theme wedding now. I'm finding myself bored at traditional weddings, so I'm thinking about unique ideas." You've explained *why* you've changed your mind and parents can make no assumptions. It's a smart thing to keep in mind if you have previously stated that you like the traditional model.

Beginning the Conversation

Once you've spent time understanding how your parents probably feel at the moment, you're ready to tell them about your plans. Follow these steps for the best chance at success:

1. **First, call each set of parents separately to make get-together plans.** You might think that the old "public place" strategy is a good idea, since parents are less likely to cause a scene with other patrons right next to you, and perhaps that feels like the best plan for you. Perhaps a lunch or dinner out at your favorite restaurant would be a great setting for this wedding chat. Or, you might feel more comfortable if you invite them to your place for a home-cooked meal or desserts, especially if your parents have *no* problem making a scene in front of strangers. The bottom line: Choose a comfortable setting.

WHEN THE WATERWORKS START . . . I hate to make generalizations, but I've found that when a parent's reactions are super-extreme, underlying regret—not getting to plan their dream wedding through you—is the culprit mindset.

2. **Keep the crowd on the small side.** It's always best to talk just with parents, rather than having your siblings, their spouses, and their kids in attendance as well, since your discussion could veer off course when your sister pipes up with her opinions, or her husband makes fun of your theme concept. The fewer judgments, the better.

3. **Bring the right materials.** Parents won't be able to fully appreciate your statement of "we'd like a casual outdoor wedding" without great visuals, so bring plenty of pages torn from bridal magazines to show them exactly what you have in mind. They might think the Crystal Ballroom in town is the best of the best, only because they've been there in the past, and they really need graphics to show them a

better way. So if you can spread out lots of pretty pictures on the dining room table, your chances of an enthusiastic reaction are far better than suggesting the idea as just a sentence. Without gorgeous photos, they may not correctly picture what you are envisioning.

4. **Have a great opener.** The right first line opens the conversation, whereas a blunt declaration like "I hope you don't think we're having a traditional wedding" stops the process before you even start. Parents would be taken aback by such a harsh statement. So choose instead any of the following wiser openings:

- "I'm so glad we're getting to work together on the wedding, and (groom) and I have decided on some really fun, unique elements for the wedding day. Here's what we have in mind . . . "
- "This is going to be so much fun working with you on the wedding! (Groom) and I have talked a lot about what we envision for our big day, what we want, what we don't want, how we want our day to be different from all the other weddings we and our guests have been to. We have some photos here to show you a bit about the style we've decided on."
- "I'm so excited to start working on the wedding with you! It's amazing to me how easily (groom) and I have decided on the basics of the day, and now we get to share those decisions with you!"
- "How fun is this? We're really excited to show you what we've decided on for the style and setting of our wedding day."

Notice there's no pre-empting, such as "I know you want us to get married in your church, *but* . . . " or any other statements that are followed by a *but*. Why even bring that up? You don't want to shine a great big spotlight on what your parents might have a problem with. Stick to the positives as your opener, and your parents might not have any problem with them at all.

Now, you'll also notice that the first three scripts are designed for a situation in which parents will be co-planning the wedding, while the fourth doesn't mention that. Part of this "breaking the news" conversation with your parents might involve more than just announcing that you're not getting married in church, like they want you to. It might be an announcement that you're planning (and paying for) the wedding on your own, which happens far more often these days as couples claim creative control over the details by paying for it themselves.

> " Giving my mother time to think about it, after she was so upset to find out we're not getting married in her church and not having a formal wedding, was the best decision possible. She called all of her friends right away—like we knew she would—and they told her to chill out and just be happy she's being invited to help plan at all. Not that we depended on *them* to persuade her, but it turned out to be a big help. " —*Nancy,* **bride-to-be**

If you're breaking the news that parents will be very minimally involved in your wedding planning, here is a good opener:

- "We know you're excited to work on the wedding plans, and we're sure you're aware that weddings are really big productions, so we've decided that we're going to follow the trend of planning the majority of the wedding ourselves, with all the parents selecting what they'd like to take on. We welcome you to let us know which items would be your favorites to work on when we get to that point, and we'll all work together to figure out how that's going to work, who will be on our 'flowers team,' for instance. We'll also bring up the tasks we'd love for you to be involved with, so we can all enjoy it together. For instance, we've already talked about how we want you to come with us to the caterer and cake tastings, and I'm sure there will be other fun stuff to do, which we'll custom-divide together. We'd be very uncomfortable having you take on a large portion of the wedding day."

You've made sure to spell out that they will be involved in much of the fun stuff, and you're going to lead the team in assigning other tasks as they come up, so you've allayed their fears there while gently claiming your rightful place as the leader. There's no easy way to break the news that parents won't be planning the entire affair when they expected and hoped to. Their reactions are going to depend on their personalities, and you may get stunned silence or you may get an argument. You might also get a relieved sigh and a big hug. You never know. Some parents will meet your announcement with a raised eyebrow, and you can imagine that *what will people think?* is cooking in their minds.

The majority of parents I spoke to in this situation worried about one thing: will our names be listed as hosts on the invitation if the bride and groom are in charge of the planning? According to Old World etiquette rules, no. But here's the great news: Today, in true bending of Old World etiquette to meet modern brides' and grooms' wishes, many couples choose to include their parents' names on the invitations anyway, in a list on a third panel or in the traditional spaces on a formal invitation, *even if they're not paying for the majority of the wedding.* That decision is up to you. Some parents' initial reactions travel from worry to disappointment and then to acceptance when you make it clear that they will be involved in some manner. It'll be a manner of your choosing, but they don't have to hear that right now.

The Heart of the Conversation

What happens next is a barrage of questions about what you've decided on for the wedding. Will it be in a church? Will it be formal? Will it be far away? Is Cousin Nettie invited? The wheels spin pretty quickly. At this point, slow them down and set the pace with, "I know you have a ton of questions, and we've surprised you with our decision to plan a (style) wedding, so let's hold off on the details for a while. Right now, all we know is that we don't want a church wedding, since that's not our style. As for the rest, we'll get to that soon." That one chunk of disappointment is probably enough for them to digest. But your delay tactic is essential. Without it, parents can get very riled up, and you'll hear all about how much you've hurt your mother and how improper it is not to have a traditional wedding.

If they continue to protest, say something like, "I can hear you're getting upset, and that's not our intention at all. I'm really sorry you're disappointed that we're not going to (insert element here), but I know you wouldn't want us to be uncomfortable or unhappy about any part of our wedding. Trust me, you're going to love what we put together. Here, look at these pictures we brought to show you what we like. It's going to be an amazing day."

If your parents are like most parents, they'll try again to push you into their vision of the day. Then, say: "I'm really sorry, but there are certain things we know we don't want. And that's one of them." Don't say *case closed* or anything else that sounds like you're an authority over them. Instead, distract. "Which part of the wedding plans do you think you might like to work on? The flowers? The cake? Why don't you take some time to think about it, and we can plan another dinner to start talking about the details?"

> " When my daughter and her fiancé told us that we weren't going to be planning the wedding, that we could pick one segment of it, I have to admit I was really stunned. And quiet. I didn't say much when they were here, and my daughter knew I was processing the information. I cried, I admit it. Because it's a parent's dream to plan a daughter's wedding. Everything . . . the white gown, the orchestra, the limousine, the whole thing. I couldn't believe I wasn't going to get to do that. But my husband told me not to ruin this time for our daughter, to look on the positive side, and just accept that I'd play a smaller role. And he really cheered me up when he told me, 'Hey, we're not going to spend $20,000 on a wedding, so let's take a cruise next summer instead.' That worked for me. " —*Annie*, **mother of the bride**

The good news for you is that this is not 1990. Unique, nontraditional weddings are not a new thing. Most parents know someone whose son or daughter planned a nontraditional if not a wacky wedding, and everything turned out well. Most parents have friends or relatives who only planned a small part of a child's wedding. Most parents are Internet-savvy, and by this point have already visited wedding websites, particularly message boards geared toward the parents of the bride and groom. So they might already have been somewhat indoctrinated into how things are for parents these days. Maybe some of the stories they read planted seeds for acceptance. Maybe they were stunned by the selfish attitudes of message board writers who railed on and on about their sons or daughters and how they refuse to attend the wedding.

These posters can be a big help to you as well, if parents have seen their missives.

Don't Expect the Worst

Believe it or not, your parents might take your news far better than you expect.

If your unique wedding plans will cost less than a traditional wedding, the financial issue will work on your side. When you can show your parents what weddings cost in your area (by visiting *www.costofwedding.com* and plugging in your zip code to see regional average expenses) they might be very happy not to spend $20,000 on the catering bill and $3,000 for a horse and carriage. Some parents—and you know yours well—hold money up as their compass, making decisions based on "how much will it cost?" Pointing out the money they'll save by letting you take the reins could be a quick, tremendous relief to all of you.

When It's Not So Easy

Clearly, not all parents will be swayed as easily as you might like, but that's no cause for panic or dismay. You simply need to be prepared with an appropriate response to their concerns. A parent's reaction might come in the form of a worry, so here are some reassuring responses:

WHEN YOU HEAR . . .	*RESPOND WITH . . .*
"But your sister's wedding was formal and traditional! Guests will think you don't have any manners!"	*"That was (sister's) style, and it was lovely. Just because we're having (element) and (element), it doesn't mean we don't have manners. It just means we have a different style. Once you see more of our plans, there will be nothing to worry about."*
"This is a wedding, not a talent show!"	*"I know it sounds unusual for us to do a tango for our first dance instead of a traditional slow dance, but it's not going to be tacky at all. We just want to add a little unexpected 'wow' factor at the start of the wedding."*
"How could you get married without the church's blessing? That's a sacrilege!"	*"We don't feel that way. I know it's something you feel very strongly about, but we've never been churchgoers, and we know that other friends haven't had any problems going to the church for future things like baby baptisms and the like. We don't consider it a sacrilege, so please see our point of view on this."*
"Having a theme wedding is going to make you look immature."	*"We've been to other theme weddings, and everyone had a terrific time because it was different and fun. We'd like to give our guests something unique to enjoy, and make the whole day a reflection of our tastes. It wouldn't be our day if it was all traditional."*
"What you have planned won't be nice enough for our guests and our colleagues to enjoy!"	*"Oh, you'd be surprised! Upper-echelon and high-society guests are the ones who started the trend of unique, themed weddings and parties, so I'm sure they'll be more pleased than you expect. Top-dollar party planners throw theme events like this one, so your guests will recognize that we're on point with the trend."*
"He put you up to this, didn't he? His family isn't the classy type, so I'm sure this is fine by them, isn't it?"	*"Wow, that was out of line. (Groom) and I decided what we want for our wedding. I wasn't pressured in any way, we're very happy with our plans, and please don't ever talk badly about my future husband or his family. That's really hurtful."*

WHEN YOU HEAR . . .	RESPOND WITH . . .
"I'm not paying for a wedding like **THAT**!"	"Oh, please don't say that! It would be such a huge disappointment if we couldn't all plan the wedding together. We don't want you to be unhappy when this is such a happy occasion. We've read so many stories online about parents who punish the bride and groom for wanting what they want. Then the wedding couples are hurt because their parents don't support their values, and the decision leads to a lifetime of regret. I know you're stunned right now, but please reconsider."
"Aunt Millie is not going to feel comfortable wearing a Halloween costume to a wedding. How can you ask your guests to do that?"	"I think you might be surprised, actually. We've been to lots of weddings and parties where guests are excited to show their creativity with their costumes. Guests can wear what they're comfortable with. Aunt Millie can just put on a big hat and be a romance writer if she'd like. Everyone's going to love the chance to have some fun in a new way, and the pictures end up hilarious. Don't worry about how people might feel. We really think everyone's going to love it."
"How can you not invite your second cousins? They invited everyone to their weddings; we have to reciprocate!"	"We thought about that, but it would open up a huge can of worms if we invited everyone from both families who has ever invited us to anything. Our guest list would be through the roof! We had to make some difficult choices. In order to keep our guest list small and affordable, we had to draw the line at first cousins. We're sure they'll understand, since most people planning weddings now are doing the same thing, sometimes to a much more severe degree. This is the best we can do."*

* **Note:** *It's not a good idea to suggest a B-list for when regrets come in, because parents tend to want everyone on that list, and it becomes a battle when No replies arrive—who "ranks highest" and gets an invitation first? Better to avoid that mess and just stand firm on the guest list you have.*

What If Parents Refuse to Help Pay?

Some parents are super-stubborn, and they're just not going to hear your pleas to reconsider their threats to withdraw their wedding contributions if you don't plan things their way. Again, you can't change people's personalities. Some parents just want to retain an iron-fist level of control over your life. Some are just not able to put your wishes first. What do you do in this case?

TRY A COMPROMISE

If your requests don't get through to them and they put up an ultimatum, your best strategy is to open up negotiations. "We stand firm on the no-church wedding, but how about if we include some religious readings like a psalm in our ceremony? We're willing to compromise with that." Many parents will smell a victory in getting you to acquiesce in some way—feeling like they've won and thus still have some control over you, and that might solve the problem. In the beginning of your planning process, the two of you discussed what's most important to you, what's at the top of your priority list, and what's not. So if you can sweeten the deal by allowing stubborn parents to take on some of your lower-priority plans like the favors or some of the after-dinner drink choices, then they may feel like you've "respected them" by giving them something they can control.

GO IT ALONE

If they're holding firm to forcing you into something that's far removed from your values, you might—sadly—have to accept their threat to remove the financial contributions, and either search for a way to boost your available funds or scale back your wedding plans with a smaller guest list or a cocktail party reception rather than a sit-down dinner. Many couples have had to adjust their plans to suit the loss of parental financial support, but they find that when they work together and keep the *meaning* in their day, the new plans they make turn out better than what they originally planned.

As the saying goes, "Necessity is the mother of invention." And if the necessity you face is planning your wedding, your way, without your parents' help, then that's simply a tough reality to face, a challenge you'll overcome together with a Plan B that still makes you very, very happy. And it's a nice way to show out-of-control parents that they can't boss you around anymore. Don't dwell on the sad fact that your parents would hurt you financially to get their way. For now, just move ahead, forgive as best you can, and focus on the fun you're still able to have planning your own, nontraditional, personalized wedding day. You have lots of supportive people around you. Keep your focus on them.

What Will Grandma Think?

Don't forget that parents are the adult children of your grandparents, and no one ever fully outgrows the fear of disappointing their parents. So some of their trepidation might come from worries about what your traditional, super-proper grandparents will think about your nontraditional wedding plans. Mom might be fine with your desire not to marry in a church or synagogue, but Grandma is going to be shocked and dismayed. And your parents may worry that *they* will get a boatload of grief from the family matriarch when they acquiesce to your wedding wishes.

Here is your solution to that dilemma. Take the onus off of your parents. Say, "I know Grandma will find our plans quite questionable, so I'll give her a call or pay her a visit to show her these same photos and invite her to participate in a craft or some-thing." The same approach as used with parents may be helpful for opinionated grandparents.

> **"**My grandmother is a tough, Eastern European widow, and she gives everyone grief about not being traditional, or not doing things the way she wants. She's been known to pout and give silent treatments, demanding her way, and my dad and his siblings always seem to give in to her. So she was my real challenge. So I visited her and played chess with her for a while, then pulled out my wedding idea book with photos to show her some of what we have in mind for the wedding. She did give me grief about our ideas, but I just said to her, 'Things are a lot different with weddings these days, and even though we won't have some of the things you'd expect, it's going to be a really wonderful day with great food and great music, lots of flowers, and dancing. You'll see . . . it's going to be a fantastic wedding. We're very happy about everything.' She sighed and put on a little drama, but it turned out okay once she realized she wasn't going to change my mind. I just smiled and brushed off her pressure tactics, changing the subject by offering to help her find the perfect dress for the occasion. **"** — *Tania,* **bride-to-be**

When the In-Laws Aren't Happy

Ah, the in-laws. It's great if you have a wonderful relationship with them, and they've embraced you as a much-loved new member of the family. You make their son happy, you get along with everyone, they love your values, maybe they even love your own family since you've all spent so much time together over the past few years.

Or, perhaps you're just starting to get to know each other. You're not entirely comfortable with their family dynamics, but you see plenty of room for growth and closeness.

Or, perhaps you're one of those brides who upsets the apple cart by jumping into their family circle, taking up your groom's time, and finding that the in-laws' personalities don't exactly mesh with yours. For some brides, sadly, there's no "Welcome" sign with the future in-laws. You bring change to their world, and they're not happy about it.

So what do you do when *his* parents are your big challenge in breaking the news that the wedding will not be the formal, traditional event they expect? Those who haven't warmed to you yet may take this announcement with a sour attitude of your wanting to "run the show." If they've interpreted any of your actions thus far as your being "in charge" of their son, they may heap on assumptions that you're overbearing. Not true and not fair. So here's how to approach *his* family with your wedding vision:

- Talk with your groom. He knows what works and what doesn't with his family, how best to break news to his parents, and how to handle their particular likes and dislikes. He may be able to warn you away from his mom's pet peeve statements, such as "it is what it is." That phrase may be quite common today, but how else would you know that she hates when people say that?

- Let your groom take the lead. He can use the starter phrases listed in this book, and he can tell his parents—with you right there by his side—that you've cocreated your wedding plan thus far, and explain why he's enthusiastic about your shared plans. Coming from his mouth, rather than yours, difficult parents wouldn't be able to brand you as the "leader" of your relationship.

- Share visuals, of course, and ask as soon as possible for his parents to participate in the manner you've planned. Invite them to let you know which portions of the day they might like to help create, which may come as a pleasant surprise to the groom's parents if they are still under the assumption that they only get to do the rehearsal dinner. Once his parents get the picture that you welcome them to shop for sites suitable for your nontraditional wedding, or taste cakes, or help design floral arrangements, they may be far more welcoming of your departures from the expected plans.

- Tackle the "her family vs. our family" issue that you've sensed lurking under the surface by letting them know, "My family is getting the same plan we're offering you, so you might get to know my parents more as you work together on some portions of the day." It may be petty, but some grooms' parents look for assurance that they're not getting the partial plan while your parents are getting to plan fully.

- Talk money. If your wedding design has you planning and paying for the wedding yourselves, look back at the script on page 73 for the same wording suggested for your parents.

- Leave the door open for their input down the road. Specifically say, "We have the basics planned, and there are going to be a lot of areas where we'll welcome your ideas down the road. It's going to be a lot of fun to work with you on this." Parents like knowing you don't have the *whole* wedding planned already, that there may be some fun in it for them later. If they push now, use the same delay strategies as described on page 74.

Hope for the Best

The bottom line is that parents don't want to ruin your wedding day. They have strong feelings, like you do, about wanting the day to be perfect, and they might not have the skills to step back and let you lead the way. Some parents still tell their adult children which outfits look good on them or where to vacation. Much depends on how well parents have differentiated themselves from their sons and daughters, if they've accepted your adult status, and if they can put your wishes above their own. A very smart closing statement is this: "We're so excited to plan a unique wedding that really reflects our ideas of fun and celebration. It's such a great thing that weddings these days are very personalized and creative, and that so many wedding vendors bring such exciting, fresh ideas to the table for a wedding that's really going to give our guests a fun time. And we all get to be in the spotlight together on that day! We couldn't be more excited."

When you show your excitement and bliss, parents recognize that you're in a state of joy—rather than a state of fear or stress—and they'll be more likely to join you there!

CHAPTER 6

Explaining Your Day to Vendors and Bridal Party Members

Everyone around you needs to understand exactly what you have in mind for your wedding day. In order for vendors to bring your creative dreams to life, and for your bridal party members to participate fully and happily, you need to communicate your wishes — and how you plan to break with tradition to have your wedding your way. While telling these people will hardly be as stressful as breaking the news to your parents, there are some *very* important factors to keep in mind from minute one. Clarity is essential for the creation of your day, especially when you plan to depart from the traditions that everyone expects. In the vast majority of cases, your vendors and your bridal party will be thrilled to hear the news. *It's not going to be a boring wedding!* They'll be eager to hear all about your plans, and they'll count themselves as lucky to get to participate in such a fun and unique celebration.

At least, that's how it will turn out most of the time. There is always the chance that some vendors and bridal party members could potentially pull out of your wedding entourage if you were to spring any surprises or changes on them midway through the process. You don't want to lose your caterer three months before the wedding because he doesn't do Thai food, nor do you want to anger your bridesmaid, who had no idea you were going to require her to fly to Hawaii for the wedding *and* perform a group dance number where she would have to wear a grass skirt with a coconut shell bra top. Personalizing your wedding is one thing—blindsiding your vendors and friends is another. So in this chapter, you're going to explore the important steps you need to take to break the news to vendors and bridal party members that this wedding will be far from what they expect.

Vendors

We're going to start off with your vendors. They are, after all, the experts and artists bringing every floral arrangement, every menu item, every frosting rose on the wedding cake to life. The key to a great wedding is having top-notch experts on your team, bringing their best talents and dedication to the table. They want to make your wedding a success, and they can do so only if you're 100 percent clear about your wedding ideas from the very start. Does this mean you can't change your mind about anything months into the planning stage? No, you have the freedom to switch from chicken to beef, or gardenias to calla lilies. What a vendor might not stand for is your dramatic switch from a traditional, indoor, ballroom, formal wedding to an outdoor, Shakespearean, alfresco buffet with tents and lighting and wandering minstrels. Especially three weeks before the wedding. Some may be able to pull it off, while others may not. After all, many vendors will make you sign a contract spelling out the terms of your agreement with them, the style and number of items you're ordering, and the services you need, and only certain degrees of change are tolerable for them. For large-scale changes, it's going to cost you. And it might cost you that expert.

Here's why: *not all vendors are willing to work on nontraditional weddings.*

IT MIGHT NOT BE TOO LATE If you've already booked your vendors and decided on packages and wedding elements, don't despair. You're not stuck with the traditional wedding you initially requested. Yes, you may have signed a contract spelling out package elements and your style, but if it's soon enough before the wedding, in the six-month to nine-month range or earlier, you may be able to start from scratch with your vendors, as if you just met them today.

It might seem silly to you that any wedding expert in today's wedding world wouldn't be willing to personalize a wedding, but there are some experts who are so busy and so set in their ways that they operate off of set package lists and set checklists *only*. They may even have it stated on their website that they only do indoor weddings, for instance. Those with equipment, such as deejays, musicians, photographers and videographers, may have a rule that they never work outdoor weddings. Period. They just can't protect their equipment out in the sun, wind, rain, or ocean salt air.

Some vendors don't work theme weddings as a matter of personal choice. Some don't work nonreligious weddings. Some won't work weddings with over 100 guests, or under fifty. Every vendor has his or her right to set boundaries and stick to them.

The way you find out about these boundaries *before you have a signed contract and guaranteed payments with these vendors* is to sit down and communicate your personalized wedding wishes in the interview stage, as you search for your vendors.

As an informed consumer, you have the right—and vendors expect today's brides and grooms—to customize what you want in your wedding package. For instance, many vendors say they often hear wedding couples call them to say, "I know I want to include a dessert buffet, but can we eliminate the soup course to make up the difference in the package price?" Many caterers will be happy to do so. Sure, deposit amounts may change when your request for a course elimination doesn't compute to an equal financial adjustment, but most of today's vendors in this economy *want* to keep your business. If you're giving them enough advance notice, they'll be happy to make the changes you want, or even start from a blank slate and help you pick fresh items to design your dream wedding day your way. Many vendors say, "I don't order the food until two months before the wedding, so I'm fine with brides' and grooms' new requests, fresh inspirations, and ideas about swapping entrées or adding some kosher or vegan foods to the cocktail party. I know the menu is important to wedding couples and their families, so I'm flexible about the changes they want to make. I'll even help them tweak the menu so that they can add the pricey seafood they originally rejected and eliminate a few other nonessential elements."

So now you have the relief of knowing you can state your nontraditional preferences most of the way through the pre-wedding months. Here are your essential steps for informing all of your vendors, in every planning category—from caterer to florist to cake baker to photographer, and so on—that you plan to depart from the traditional, expected wedding model, to really mix things up and get creative for your wedding, planned your way:

IF YOU'VE ALREADY BOOKED

If you've already booked your vendor for a traditional wedding and have since changed your mind about some or all of the elements, get on the phone immediately and request an in-person meeting where you will explain your new style and plans. Don't delay out of fear, as some couples do. When you share your new style wishes, the vendor will either assure you that he or she can fulfill your wishes or—if the vendor can't work with you—suggest a talented colleague for you to contact, research, and interview. The more time you give for a changing of the guard, the better.

IF YOU HAVEN'T BOOKED

If you haven't booked your vendors yet, start by asking friends for referrals to experts who created weddings or corporate events, family parties, fundraisers, or other big get-togethers in a similar style to yours. When you have your list of candidates, embark on the "consultation tour"—make appointments for free consultations with vendors—and the good ones do *not* charge for an initial, informational meeting—and share your wish list with them. When you walk in, don't just launch into the A to Z list of what you want for your wedding. Assess the vibe between the two of you. Is this vendor really present with you, listening to you, eager to see your materials, or is she answering phones and multitasking? Do you get the sense that she's overwhelmed? The most important factor in connecting with the one great vendor who will bring your personalized wedding plans into fruition is that he or she is a great match for *you*. You'll be able to feel that as you proceed into explaining what and when your wedding will be. At the end of this section, you'll find a worksheet that you can hand each vendor, giving them the concrete information they need to fully grasp your style. From there, you go to the next step . . . .

GATHER MATERIALS TO SHOW YOUR STYLE

These would be torn-out photo spreads from bridal magazines, printouts from floral or cake websites, even celebrity wedding magazines. Point out your desired style for an all-natural, lush, outdoor wedding reminiscent of the Tuscan countryside, or whatever your choice is. Vendors will better understand your style when they have visuals to work with. "This scene of the outdoor tapas party inspired our design for the cocktail party," you might explain. "And then we'd like everyone to move into a tent designed"—flip to the graphic you brought along—"like this one, filled with flowers and lots of white fabrics and spotlights." If you can show them images from their *own* website, such as that gorgeous photo of the cocktail party station that caught your eye, the vendor will be better able to re-create and tweak that design for you.

SHARE YOUR *DON'T* LIST

Your Don't List should include things such as the foods you don't want, the floral designs you don't want, the types of photos you don't want, and so on. Vendors say they learn just as much vital information from a wedding couple by knowing what they hate, as well as what they love. Visit my website, *www.sharonnaylor.net*, to get your free copies of Don't List worksheets to bring to your vendors, and fill them out together so that each of your "don'ts" are fully recorded.

EXPLAIN WHERE YOUR STYLE DIFFERS FROM YOUR GROOM'S

Wedding vendors are experts not only at styling the mediums they work in, but in working magic with planning groups. They have plenty of experience in hearing two disparate wishes for, say, table-setting design, and suggesting the perfect compromises.

Wedding experts *love* it when you're open and honest about the places where the two of you don't agree. They enjoy taking on the challenge of leading you both to a happy middle point where each of your wishes are heard and respected. Many vendors say they ask wedding couples for a *third* option that departs from both sides' original visions. For instance, if you want a white tablecloth and your groom wants a dark green tablecloth and neither of you want to budge, that vendor might ask you to pick another color that you've used in your floral centerpieces, such as a dark rose color with both white and dark green accents in the additional florals and the designs of the china place settings. Or she may be able to show you a dark green tablecloth with a gossamer white table runner to get you the best of both worlds. Most couples aren't even aware that table runners are an option; problem solved!

LIST THE CONFLICTS YOU'RE HAVING WITH YOUR PARENTS

If parents are paying for all or part of the wedding, or if they will be working firsthand with your wedding vendors as well, it's ultra-important that your vendors hear directly from you what the conflict is. Now, here's where it gets interesting. You might want your vendor to take your side 100 percent of the time, but don't be surprised if your vendor says, "Actually, in this case, given the architectural details of the ballroom, I think your mother's choice of elevated floral centerpieces for each table is going to be the most flattering." The vendor will explain why: "An elevated centerpiece draws the eye up, extending your décor to 'fill the room.' Other-wise, with the low-set peonies you're thinking about, that would leave over two-thirds of the room essentially empty. The room would look cavernous and underdecorated."

And from here . . . you work with the vendor to bring your wished-for elements—like those peonies—into an expert-led compromise that still allows you to tweak a traditional centerpiece choice. Mom might not have thought about tall, flowering cherry blossom branches to give even more height to the centerpieces, so in talking to your vendor about the traditional-versus-nontraditional conflict you have going on, you've just reached a far more gorgeous option.

YOUR VENDOR WORKS MIRACLES Vendors know just what to say when a parent is proving difficult or stressful to you. He or she might say to them, "I know (your names) have planned their wedding in a style you didn't expect, but I know you're going to be very happy with the results. It's going to be lovely and elegant, and best of all, it's going to make the bride and groom very, very happy." Vendors also say they like to shock parents a little bit. "I know exactly where you're coming from when you see these plans for a theme wedding. I've had so many parents in here who were upset about the plans, and acted so horribly toward the bride and groom that they ruined their relationships with the couple and with the in-laws. No holidays, limited time with the grandkids in the future, no family vacations . . . all because they had to put up a fight over having sushi at the cocktail party! It's just so sad to see families not think about what this time means for the future." Parents really listen to objective third-party advisors when it comes to the grandkids!

Tell your vendors about *fundamental* conflicts you're having with your parents. Sometimes, the argument is not about peonies and flowering branches, but much larger challenges. "My parents really want us to get married in a church, which we're not going to do, so they threatened not to come to the wedding." Vendors hear this one, unfortunately, all the time, and while they won't be able to wave a magic wand and make all sides get along, they *will* be able to speak and work with the parents using a reassuring tone, presenting to them (after conferring with you) some planning details the parents might wish to work on. Wedding vendors of all types are actually people persons, with years of experience in charming parents into better moods and mindsets, and they are quite skilled at knowing how to get right to the solution without sharing too much extra information that might send parents spiraling into a fresh, new conflict about the centerpieces, for instance. You'll find that those who have been in the wedding industry for a long time have terrific problem-solving skills in planning groups, so you basically get an expert mediator as part of your plan!

BE CONSCIOUS OF THE TIME THE VENDOR WILL NEED TO FULFILL YOUR PLANS

This is especially important if you are now adding some changes to the original package you booked, to any degree. A vendor looks at your initial choices and the time it will take to build arches or make thirty appetizer choices or bake a six-tiered cake, and then decides how much time will need to be devoted to your wedding in the weeks prior, as well as on the wedding day. Since many vendors book multiple weddings per weekend, each with a certain number of prep hours blocked off, your new requested changes could put quite a squeeze on them. Some vendors will tell you, again, that the new scope of your plans may not be possible. Some will bring in extra workers to bring your wishes to life. Remember that *many* hours go into everything you're ordering, and that's often your vendor's first concern. It's actually the good ones who will tell you that they can't stretch themselves that thin without your wedding elements suffering. So it's a great move on your part to show that you're taking their time into consideration by asking, "If we add theme backdrops and extra lighting, how much extra time does that take for you?"

GIVE AN EXAMPLE Here's another insider secret: arm your vendors with the one "comparison story" that will really impact your parents, such as, "(Bride and groom) tell me that Cousin Amy had a 400-person, traditional wedding at a ballroom where the catering was just blah, and that relatives are still talking about how disappointing the food was. That's part of why (your names) want to pay special attention to the menu choices." Parents are competitive, and they have "what will people think?" coded into their DNA. When a vendor lobs this one at them, parents become open to new ideas quickly.

REQUEST FLUID WORDING IN YOUR CONTRACT

If your wedding plans are at a point where you know the basics of what you want, but you still want the freedom and ability to add some new elements later, ask for an addendum to that vendor's detailed contract allowing for "approved modifications" to be set within x number of weeks before the wedding. Most vendors will want sixty to ninety days at least, and some will want more if they order their materials and supplies from overseas vendors. That means flowers, fabrics, and other materials that—like it or not in our age of Made in the U.S.A.—may cost you less. But they do need time for ordering and shipping, plus time to craft your requested masterpieces.

SHOW YOUR UNDERSTANDING OF THE MARKET

A caterer may shop at organic markets, a floral designer may shop at an organic wholesaler. A photographer may work with a company that makes albums out of eco-friendly materials. Do your research well, ask plenty of questions, and understand that when you order eco-friendly items, prices often go up. Your requests may require an increase in your price package, and vendors want to work with couples who can accept that, not those who want to fight them in a nickel-and-dime battle on every little thing.

Vendors' Stories

Basics aside, vendors share some insider stories of what you can better do to explain your style to them:

- "When a bride told me that she didn't like the lineup poses that are the usuals for groups of bridesmaids and the bridal party, I knew to plan for an extra half hour of getting candid photos of the bride and her bridesmaids while they were getting ready for the wedding. Then I did the same with the groom and his men before the ceremony started, and again with the entire bridal party group as they mingled after the ceremony itself. The result was photos that were exactly what the couple wanted, more natural and less stiff poses, the real interactions between them captured for their albums."—Renata, photographer

- "I love it when couples write on printouts of the images they like. One couple printed out pictures of three different wedding cakes they saw on a bridal website, and they wrote on those pictures, 'LOVE the icing beading look!' and 'Pink flowers, not yellow,' and 'Daisies on the fronts of each layer, not on the top.' You *are* allowed to give a vendor this kind of detailed information. Don't worry about seeming bossy. I want these kinds of notes."—Desiree, cake baker

- "Don't just say you want a nontraditional wedding. Show me exactly how you want it different."—Jake, caterer

- "When you walk into my studio, I'm checking you out to assess your style. I can tell by looking at your shoes, your handbag, your jewelry, your makeup and how you speak with your groom so much about you, and my goal is to bring you into your wedding plans."—Sheila, wedding coordinator

- "I make it clear at the outset . . . I don't care if parents are paying for the wedding. The bride and groom are my clients. So I take orders only from them, not from parents calling me to change their plans behind their backs. When it's a nontraditional wedding, I get a lot of ultratraditional parents pulling the 'I'm paying for it' move and thinking they can change the wording on invitations or the style of the programs. Make sure you tell your vendors that you are the contact person for every wedding decision, and that if parents call them to make a change, nothing is to be done without your approval. Some parents are nervy and they may just do something sneaky rather than ask permission. So close the door on that potential problem by telling your vendors that you're in charge."—Leah, invitations designer

Your Style Worksheet

Fill this worksheet out together and make plenty of copies in order to give them out to all of your wedding vendors for safekeeping in your client folder. Vendors want to know what you're doing in *every* category so that their part of the day coordinates with what other vendors will be doing.

Your Names: _____

Contact Information: _____

Wedding Date: _____

Ceremony

Ceremony Time: _____

Ceremony Location: _____

Indoor or Outdoor Ceremony: _____

Wedding Color Theme: _____

Theme Wedding Style: _____

Religious Elements: _____

Cultural Elements: _____

Décor Desired: _____

Ceremony Elements: _____

Ceremony Tone: _____

Cocktail Party

Cocktail Party Planned? Yes / No

Cocktail Party Time and Location:_____

Indoor or Outdoor: _____

Cocktail Party Style: _____

Cocktail Party Theme: _____

Menu Wish List: _____

Reception

Reception Style: _____

Indoor or Outdoor: _____

Reception Elements Desired: _____

Reception Menu Desired: _____

Reception Menu Restrictions: _____

Cake Style: _____

Desserts Style: _____

Drink Style: _____

Entertainment Style: _____

Wedding Details

Floral and Décor Style: _____

Photo and Video Style: _____

Transportation Style: _____

Dress Style for Bride: _____

Dress Style for Bridesmaids:_____

Number of Bridesmaids: _____

Wardrobe Style for Groom: _____

Wardrobe Style for Groomsmen: _____

Number of Groomsmen: _____

Child Attendants' Style: _____

Number of Child Attendants:_____

Tributes and Special Dances: _____

Favors: _____

Additional Notes (Attach your Don't List, by category, here for your vendor's review.)

_____

_____

_____

_____

_____

Explaining Your Day to Bridal Party Members

When you ask a friend or relative to participate in your bridal party, they obviously need to know the what, where, and when for the wedding day, and your most excited friends and family members in your inner circle will certainly ask about the details of your day. In this age of personalized weddings, bridesmaids and groomsmen know that their parts of the day can now go far beyond "what will we be wearing?" In years past, bridesmaids feared the peach dress with the puffy sleeves and the hoop skirt. Groomsmen really didn't care much unless you wanted them in pink ties and vests à la 1980s proms. But now, with television shows depicting bridal parties doing the dance number from Michael Jackson's *Thriller* or being asked to *ski* down a mountain slope as the processional, savvy bridal parties know they may be in for an adventure.

> " When my sister said she was having a Renaissance-themed wedding in the woods, I immediately Googled costume rentals for those heaving-bosom bodice dresses and almost passed out when I saw they were over $300. But that was just my imagination running away. My sister called right away to say, 'No period costumes. I'd like you all in pink gowns from the Dessy Collection, with floral wreaths on your heads and a single flower as your bouquet.' Once she gave me the visual, I calmed down. " —*Anita*, maid of honor

DEALING WITH COSTS

One thing hasn't changed: bridal parties want to know one big thing: *What is this going to cost me?* That's a universal concern for all bridal party members at any type of wedding, but when you break the news that yours will be nontraditional, bridesmaids and groomsmen may hear a cash register sound effect and fret about increased expenses for theme-wedding costumes or a long flight to Tahiti. Before your inner circle panics—which often leads to phone calls, e-mails, and text messages for reassurance that they won't be asked to sacrifice too much in your honor (although they'd never say it exactly like that!)—be sure to communicate to each of them exactly what will be expected of them. It could be that your personalized wedding plans won't affect them at all. Their roles, in group decisions on a classic bridesmaid dress or booking their travel arrangements for your wedding weekend, could remain untouched by your creative flourishes on your wedding day. The fun and unique elements might be in the food and entertainment categories only.

Yes, bridal party members can freak out, especially with so many stories online about so-called quirky weddings where the bride and groom don't seem to *like* their bridal party members too much! An underwater scuba wedding, when bridal party members either haven't been accredited for scuba, or don't like the water? A wedding where the bridesmaids and groomsmen are asked to dress up like clowns, complete with big red wigs and noses? A Vegas wedding where bridesmaids are commanded to wear skimpy Vegas showgirl thongs and bras with fishnet stockings and big feather headdresses? It's all out there online, ready to scare the life out of your bridal party. So that's why you want to avoid just saying, "We're going to have a really unique, fun, out-there wedding unlike any you've ever seen before!"

BE UP FRONT ABOUT PLANS

Bridal parties do *not* find it fun to wait for your next announcement. They haven't signed on for a reality show where embarrassing oneself is the norm. They agreed to be in your wedding, and they don't want to be pressured into humiliating costumes or skits that will make it difficult for them to run for public office someday. So here's rule number one:

Give bridal party members full details on your nontraditional wedding right from the start, and let them decide if they want to participate or not.

This early in the process, if a bridesmaid wants to step down, you will honor her decision and perhaps add a new bridesmaid to your group. Now let's look a little deeper into the whole "resigning from the bridal party" issue. It *is* a big deal, and a possibility whenever you inform wedding participants that you will be asking them to take on nontraditional roles or participate in nontraditional rituals. Some bridal party members may have strong beliefs about religion and weddings, and when they hear there will be little to no religious element in your ceremony, they may not feel right about participating. Some are shy by nature and wouldn't feel comfortable playing the part of a "performer" in a theme wedding—it's just not their style. They weren't expecting to be in a show. They were expecting to walk in your processional, stand up for you during the ceremony, and walk in the recessional. When you originally asked them to be in your bridal party, that's what they expected.

That's the key word here: expectations. And just like you wouldn't safely change plans with a vendor when he or she has expectations of creating a certain kind of floral design, menu, entertainment plan, or dress for you, you can't guarantee a good outcome if you vastly counter what your bridal party members' expectations are. The only remedy to this is spelling out the following to them as soon as possible, see page 104 for a list of these expectations.

1. **The style of your wedding.** "We've decided to have our wedding outdoors as a country theme, rather than a formal ballroom wedding."

2. **Your plans for their wardrobe.** "Even with our theme wedding, you'll still be in the exact same kind of formal gown you would wear to a traditional wedding, only we'll have you carry a Mardi Gras mask on a stick rather than a floral bouquet." Men can be told, "We're not going with tuxes. All of the guys will be in khaki pants and white button-down shirts with a coral-colored tee shirt underneath."

3. **Your plans to save them money.** "Costumes run about $300 for a rental, so we're going to have you wear pretty formal dresses from Ann Taylor for under $100, and we'll add a sash and some hair accessories to give your look a Vegas style." This issue is very important to your bridal party, since they may be spending a lot for their travel and lodging.

> " Since our theme wedding was going to require a slight bit more of a financial investment from our bridal party, we both told our groups to *forget* about giving us bachelor and bachelorette parties. We didn't want them, and we wanted to give our bridal parties a financial break. We told them this right at the beginning, so they really were quite happy to know they wouldn't have to spend hundreds each for an extra party. " —*Danielle,* **newlywed**

4. **Let them know about the date you've chosen**. It sounds like a basic thing, the When of the wedding. But if you've chosen a holiday weekend, or a popular vacation week such as winter break or peak summer months, your bridal

party members need to know when to plan to be with you with plenty of advance notice so that they don't book (and have to cancel) their annual family vacations. Also, let them know about any essential pre-wedding meetings, including your wish to get together with your bridesmaids once a month to go over wedding-related planning.

5. **Let them know which early steps they need to take.** Like getting a passport so that they can join you at your destination wedding. Help them with this task, such as sending them a link to the government's passport website section and letting them know which area post offices process passport applications.

6. **Let them know the roles they'll play at the wedding.** "We'd like our bridal party members to dress up in costume for our Halloween-themed wedding, and instead of being with us before the ceremony, be outside at the reception site to greet the guests."

7. **Let them know you're willing to customize their roles.** If a bridesmaid doesn't like the idea of standing outside to be spooky with guests, let her know that she and other bridesmaids can stand up on the balcony and just wave down to the guests. Always show that you're willing to meet their comfort level. "How can we tweak your role so that you're more comfortable?" is a great way to give your bridal party members some control over their "character" and placement, while still including them in your grand plan for a creative experience.

8. **Ask them if they have any concepts or connections.** Forget about wanting to make every decision yourselves. Your friends and family might suggest the perfect theme item for

table centerpieces, or they might know of the perfect musicians to suit the theme for the cocktail party. They might say, "I have an unbelievable craft store near my house, so be sure to check there for your décor items. And since I'm a member of their rewards program, I can give you all the coupons I have."

WHEN THEY SAY "I DON'T GET IT"

It can be shocking when you're sitting in front of your most fun-loving bridesmaid, excitedly sharing the details of your theme wedding, and she has one eyebrow raised as she says, "I don't get it." Or she delivers the dreaded "Are you *sure*?" which can throw you off-balance if you're even slightly nervous about breaking with tradition for your wedding. Yes, parents may question your judgment, but when that look of disapproval comes from your *friend*, that can sting.

DON'T TAKE IT PERSONALLY It's a *huge* mistake to get offended or shut down when your bridal party members suggest possibilities for your theme or nontraditional wedding. The minute you tell them this wedding is going to be unique, their imaginations may spring into action *for your benefit.* If you're feeling overwhelmed—which can happen with too much *good* stuff going on at once, too—the excited suggestions of a loved one can feel like pressure. If bridal party members start making suggestions right now, just tell them to "hold that thought" for later-stage plan discussions. It's okay to admit that your head is spinning with so much going on right now.

To help you keep from spiraling out, losing your nerve, and veering back into the traditional wedding category, let me share a few bridal party stories with you:

- "When my friend said she was going to have a sports-themed reception, my first thought was 'that's *so* not her! She's just agreeing to it to make her fiancé happy.' I was pretty rude about it, too. The bottom line was that while we've been friends forever, I live halfway across the country, and I didn't know how much she had grown to love football over the years she'd been with him. So, she explained, this wedding theme was very much 'her.' In fact, she suggested the concept to her fiancé. I chalk my initial hesitation up to being protective of her, but I can see now that I was just overreacting based on an assumption I had no business making."—Claire, recent bridesmaid

- "I'll never forget how crushed my friend the bride was when I laughed at her wedding plans when she first told me about her spiritual wedding on a mountaintop. I always knew she was involved with a spiritual community, but some of the details she was talking about seemed a little too wacky to me. You can apologize, but you can never take it back when your first reaction at a big moment actually turns out to be cruel. Our relationship is strained now, so all I can say is this . . . if a friend laughs at your plans, please know that people react badly based on whatever mindset they're in. I can tell you that I was feeling lousy because it seemed like all of my friends were getting married, and I couldn't find a good guy at all. Some friends are distracted and think you're joking when you surprise them with things they don't expect."—Michaela, upcoming bridesmaid . . . maybe

- "Why did I laugh at my sister's wedding plans? Because I'm jealous like you wouldn't believe. She gets everything she wants, and now I have to stand there and smile while she gets even more? If by laughing at her plans for a Great Gatsby outdoor wedding I can take her down a few notches, and thus narrow the huge gap between what she has and what I have, I'm going to laugh my butt off."—Totally fictional Evil Bridesmaid, showing you that obligatory bridal party invitations are a really bad idea, and that mocking of your wedding plans shouldn't be taken seriously.

WHEN YOU GET REPEATED WARNINGS

If many of your bridal party members cringe when you tell them about your personalized wedding plans, not because they don't want to wear a costume or participate in a cultural ceremony but because they question the taste level of your idea, now is not the time to dig in your heels and scream, "I want it my way!" Your most trusted friends and family members are going to mention it to you if they feel your creativity could cross a line of decency as understood in your community and family.

As one exaggerated example, if you are heavily involved in a certain political party or environmental group, it could seem like you're preaching to your guests if you include over-the-top signs and messages about government policy or logging as a part of your wedding. While you believe strongly in your causes, your guests will likely be offended if what you've really invited them to is a rally or fundraiser for a group *they* don't support. And if there are speeches, you've just made them a captive audience. Friends and family who hear your plans for this kind of "advocacy" or "message" wedding will want to risk a confrontation with you in your best interest. They don't want you to burn bridges, which isn't a good idea for the environment. Keep an open mind, talk to an uninvolved third party such as a religious counselor or a trusted mentor, and figure out how to scale back your initial ideas.

So what are you supposed to say when friends voice their concern, amusement, or disdain for your plans: *"Just wait and see . . . it's going to be fantastic!"*

Part Three

PUTTING IT TOGETHER FOR LESS

There's no doubt about it, weddings are expensive. And depending on your personal selections and tastes for luxury, your theme wedding plans and personalization steps, you might find some areas of your wedding climbing to staggering prices. The chapters in this section will help you "beat the system" and plan your wished-for wedding elements for less.

CHAPTER 7

Budget-Minded Ways to Break Tradition

While there are literally thousands of ways to save money on your dream wedding plans, I've included the top five in each of the main bridal categories. As you're exploring your wedding themes and color schemes, tastes and textures, and as the freedom you now have to plan your wedding your way opens up new doors and new creative opportunities, you're probably finding that the *cost* of the wedding is getting scary. All these fabulous theme ideas and personalization concepts come with a price tag, after all, and your innovative plans for entertainment might cost three times the price of a designer wedding gown.

First Things First

Have you hit a brick wall? Is the *money* the new enemy to planning your wedding your way? You overcame parental limits, and now you have to face financial limits? Don't panic. Your personalized plans are not in peril when you take the following smart steps as the foundation of your smart shopping and spending plans:

1. **Build your priority list.** Which wedding elements are most important to you—the food, the entertainment, the photos? That's where you'll devote the largest percentage of your available budget, and you might even decide to spare no expense in these areas. For your lower priorities, say, invitations and a big dessert spread, you'll cut those budget allowances in half—or cut out the big dessert spread altogether. Let them eat cake .. . and strawberries. With these smart budget-focus plans, you won't have to sacrifice quality on your top wedding wishes.

2. **Work your network.** Who do you know in any fields, at any locations, who can pass along savings to you, or hook you up with a freebie?

3. **Take advantage of seasonal sales.** Before the winter gift-giving holidays, you'll find *big* sales at most of your favorite stores, sometimes 60 percent to 70 percent off. Those stores want to post great sales figures, so they're enticing shoppers with killer savings. Even if your wedding is nine months away, shop now for décor items or your wedding gown, shoes, invitations, favors, and so on. Find postholiday sales or end-of-summer sales as well, net big discounts on anything you need.

4. **Borrow from family and friends.** It might be strings of white lights for décor, china settings for the rehearsal dinner, even a wedding gown. *Something borrowed* is in that age-old tradition for a reason! The more you can borrow, the more you personalize *and* add sentimentality to your wedding at the same time. And since you're doing your wedding your way, there may be creative items you can borrow, such as cobalt blue platters for your sea-themed reception

or potted palm trees from the neighbor's yard to set out as décor for your backyard tropical-themed wedding.

Save in Each Section

Now let's get into the top five planning tips for each section of your wedding plans, with a reminder that creative budget-saving plans often open up greater opportunities to plan your wedding your way. You're not just choosing menu items off a caterers' checklist or ordering a ready-to-wear gown from a bridal shop—you're not accepting what is placed in front of you as "the way it's done." You do have options to make *everything* your personal style, so here's a primer on money-saving ways to bring more creativity into your plans:

TIMING

The time of year can have perhaps the most significant impact on your overall budget.

1. Pick a Less Expensive Time of Year

Set your wedding date outside of peak wedding season, which usually runs from May to September and is the time when wedding prices may be double or triple the fees charged *outside* of peak wedding months. April may be the perfect month for weather and spring colors, and at one-third the price of a September wedding, your money will go much further in bringing your personalized plans to life. In planning your wedding your way, you might be thrilled to find that your favorite season—spring—means that the grounds of your wedding location will be blooming with plenty of tulips and daffodils for an extra-special *free* décor plan!

2. Choose an Off-Peak Time of Day

Look at different weekend time slots, such as a 1 P.M. Saturday formal wedding, which is identical to the 7 P.M. or 8 P.M. wedding that's costing way more. Or hold a Sunday afternoon wedding, again identical to the Saturday night wedding but costing far less. Friday nights are often priced at 10 percent to 20 percent less than Saturday nights as well, but by virtue of being nighttime affairs they bring an etiquette responsibility to be more formal events.

3. Serve a Lighter Meal

The time of day may allow you to hold a wedding luncheon or cocktail party, a breakfast, or—saving you from the Friday night formal sit-down dinner—a dessert and champagne party. If the evening sit-down dinner reception and dancing into the night is not your preference, perhaps an earlier-in-the-day cocktail party with light hors d'oeuvres and champagne suits your style and saves you 50 percent to 60 percent per guest. Couples who book morning weddings say they get the classy, elegant affair they wanted, no one's getting drunk, food is lighter and refreshing, an outdoor reception takes place in the warmer hours of the day . . . it all fulfills their wedding dream. Plus, you might find that it's going to be far more fun for your family members, including the elder generations, to party during the daytime, rather than expect them to dance at a 9 P.M. wedding reception when they're usually fast asleep by 9 P.M.

4. Assess Your Level of Formality

Formality rules are important to discuss, since a formal wedding requires a certain level of propriety in décor, dress, invitations, and menu. Are you a more casual couple who would enjoy a less formal wedding? Perhaps an afternoon wedding that avoids having to serve a full dinner at the dinnertime hours of a 5 P.M. to 7 P.M. reception? Guests take their etiquette seriously, and they will expect a big meal at dinnertime. It's a travesty to serve informal and skimpy portions in the dinner hours. This is one of those obligations that still hold strong. So if you're looking at evening timing and leaning toward a more formal wedding, be prepared to have your elements live up to the standards.

5. Take Time to Plan

Allow yourselves plenty of time to plan your wedding. Fourteen months is the national average, according to TheWedding Report.com, and having a good year to plan allows you to hit seasonal sales for great bargains and more creative opportunities. Plus, you'll avoid planning in a rush and potentially booking substandard vendors or making hasty decisions. Can you plan a wedding in under six months? Yes, absolutely. But you would miss half a year's worth of seasonal and store sales *and* add an element of intensity to the planning and creation of your wedding elements. Decide if you *like* a speedy pace, if you want to just get to the part where you're married, and set your date accordingly.

LOCATION

With a plethora of locations available to host weddings these days, you can find a location to fit any budget.

1. Check the Site's Rules

Choose a site that doesn't have restrictions, such as not allowing tents to be set up on their grounds, or requirements to book their vendors. These sites want to keep a tight rein on how weddings are planned, and you don't want to be controlled or limited when your goal is to plan your wedding your way. You need the flexibility to bring in cheaper options, too.

2. Don't Drown in Add-Ons

Unique sites are attractive to couples who want to plan their own unique weddings, but avoid those that don't have their own supplies of tables, chairs, and other essentials. You might find a great museum or arboretum for your dream wedding setting, but if you have to rent thousands of dollars worth of fundamentals, the drain on your budget might take away from the money you need to fulfill other elements of your dream wedding. If you're having a small wedding, you might decide to bring in your own tablecloths, serving platters, and china sets, as both a way to save money and insert more personalization into your day.

3. Look Off the Beaten Path

Check with a wedding coordinator (*www.bridalassn.com*) or your local tourism department (*www.towd.com*) to discover terrific, little-known event locations such as estate homes that can be rented out for weddings. These professionals know every site in town, and you may find that dreamy mansion that's perfect for your Great Gatsby–style theme wedding.

4. Negotiate

If you prefer holding your wedding in a hotel ballroom, keeping the event close to where guests are staying, remind yourself that you *can* request changes to the caterer's standard wedding-package printouts. They want to make you happy, so put on your Skilled Negotiator hat and arrange for the customizations you want and the trades you'd like to achieve, such as eliminating their international coffee bar and adding an extra station to the cocktail party.

5. Keep the Destination Close

Want a destination wedding, but worry that requiring parents and grandparents and friends to fly to an island would be too much for them? Plan a destination wedding that's just an hour or two away, perhaps in wine country or at a shore resort town, a mountain lodge, or other unique location. You may find the perfect place that offers lower rates than your hometown banquet halls and still allows everyone to "escape" without the hassle and expense of flying. Plus, the location you choose could be one of special sentimentality, such as the shore or ski town where your family has vacationed year after year. Again, check out *www.towd.com* to find the local tourism departments in regions you're considering.

GUEST LIST

Some couples feel that the guest list is open to negotiation; others don't. Here are some options to consider.

1. Keep It Short

Say no to extended relatives you don't know, parents' friends you don't know, and all additional "obligatory" invites. Parents tend to get grabby about wedding guest lists, wanting to include larger groups of guests who are important to them, so exercise those "no" muscles by limiting the guest list to those most important to you.

2. Don't Invite the +1s

It's okay to leave "and guest" off of your invites for single guests. These days, it's quite common for brides and grooms to chop out the dreaded +1s, and single guests have come to accept that they can't always bring a rent-a-date. Make it a rule: if you don't know a guest's significant other already (such as the case of a longtime boyfriend you've met and socialized with), it's a no to the +1. A great way to enforce this rule when guests *ask* why their new boyfriend isn't invited is to say, "We had to limit the +1s to couples with whom we've socialized, where we're friends with both partners. It was a very difficult decision to make, but our space and budget concerns made this a necessity. We hope you understand."

3. Limit Parents' Special Guests

Limit parents' guest lists to five or so guests each, which is quite thoughtful of you, and prevents parents' push for thirty of their friends with whom they exchange holiday cards only.

4. Don't Invite Kids

It's okay to say no to kids, unless a full-family event is a high priority of yours. But check with the site: many don't charge for kids under ten years old.

5. Whittle Down the List of Coworkers

Resist the temptation to invite entire groups of colleagues. Limit your list to only those with whom you socialize outside of the office. Again, people know weddings are expensive and they'll understand your space and budget constraints.

RECEPTION FOOD

You do have to serve food at your reception, of course, but no one says it has to be a six-course surf-and-turf extravaganza!

1. Pass Hors d'Oeuvres Rather Than Use Buffet Style

Have pricier menu options, such as shrimp cocktail and scallops, hand-passed by servers during the cocktail party instead of setting them out on a buffet table, which limits consumption and saves you up to 40 percent. If you want a VIP flair for your wedding, having white-gloved servers presenting silver platters of hors d'oeuvres to your guests definitely suits that style. Most sites include the services of their waitstaff in the wedding package, but don't assume that's the case. Ask if there's a per-server charge and if you can negotiate it out of the contract due to the size and scope of your wedding. Again, most site managers are happy to throw you such discounts when you ask.

2. Consider Your Entrées Carefully

Choose inexpensive entrée options such as chicken and pasta, and have your caterer prepare them gourmet-style with unique sauces and garnishes to make them look more expensive.

3. Cut Out the Choice

Present guests with a combination platter entrée consisting of a few grilled shrimp and beef medallions instead of giving them their choice of three different entrée options. The chef then knows exactly how much food to buy and doesn't have to triple the shopping list to allow guests to switch their choices. This can save as much as 40 percent off your food bill.

4. Eat More Veggies!

Include more vegetarian options in your menu, which saves a fortune and pleases you and/or your non-meat-eating guests.

5. Eliminate a Course

Eliminate a course from the reception meal, such as a pasta or salad, since guests likely enjoyed those types of food at the cocktail hour, and eliminate one food station from the cocktail party. Make sure your remaining stations are unique and pleasing, including foods guests don't get at every other wedding. By having different types of foods, it will look like you spent more when in fact you have saved.

DRINKS

The beverages you serve can be quite affordable if you plan ahead, but they can spiral out of control if you don't.

1. Limit the Choices

Limit the number of drinks served at the bar, such as a selection of wines, beers, and two or three types of mixed drinks, rather than a completely open bar with every type of liquor available.

2. Offer a Signature Cocktail

Plan for flavorful sangrias and a *selection* of three or four signature cocktails to present variety while avoiding the expense of offering a full, open bar with every cocktail imaginable. A signature cocktail is a surefire way to personalize your wedding your way, especially when you choose a drink that's your favorite, or name the drink after yourselves.

3. Cut Out the Heavy Stuff

Don't offer shots and multiliquor drinks such as Long Island iced teas to cut down on the amount of liquor you'll have to pay for.

4. Do Some Research

Check *www.winespectator.com* to learn about award-winning, lower-priced wines and champagnes that you can supply or request for your wedding. To create your wine list your way, research vintages from your favorite region or country, or select the same type of wine you enjoyed when you got engaged.

5. Emphasize Nonalcoholic Options

Provide plenty of creative soft drink and iced tea options, which cost less and please guests . . . especially on a hot day. If a mixture of lemonade and iced tea is your own favorite soft drink refresher, add that to your drink menu.

CAKE AND DESSERTS

Your guests will certainly be expecting some delicious desserts—but again, you can offer treats that are delicious and affordable.

1. Take It Down a Tier

Have a three-tier wedding cake instead of a five-tier cake. Cut the smaller one, and have the site serve your guests from that and from a sheet cake back in the kitchen.

2. Keep It Simple

Choose less ornate décor for your cake, since it's the labor of intricate icing and sugar-paste flowers that ramps up the cost of cakes. A smooth icing, rather than an intricate dot pattern or sugar-paste ribbons and flowers, is elegant and looks more expensive than it is.

3. Stick to the Basics

Choose from the site's list of standard cake flavors and fillings, rather than their list of extra-cost flavors like cannoli cream and rum cream fillings. You *can* request different cake and filling flavor pairings for each cake layer, often at little to no extra cost, which gives guests their choice of, say, chocolate cake with chocolate mousse or traditional vanilla cake with strawberries and buttercream frosting. When you and your groom can't agree upon a single cake flavor combo, this is your best solution.

4. Use a Fancy Sauce

Dress up a standard-flavor cake such as vanilla cake with strawberry filling by providing a vanilla dessert sauce on the side. If you have a favorite dessert sauce, such as caramel, white chocolate, dark chocolate, or berry, order those as the side sauces to personalize your cake's presentation while still saving money.

5. Limit the Choices

Skip the enormous dessert table and just serve wedding cake and chocolate-dipped strawberries or petit fours. These elegant choices make just as great an impression as a lineup of pies, tarts, and mousses. One hot trend to partner with a cake is a gelato bar offering two to three different flavors of homemade frozen treats, or a unique dessert station such as mini Belgian waffles with vanilla ice cream and fresh whipped cream—offering guests something they don't get at every other wedding. A quick tip: ask if you can have two to three Belgian waffle stations in separate corners of the room so that a gigantic line doesn't keep guests waiting too long.

ENTERTAINMENT

Your entertainment may be an area where you're looking to customize your wedding. Here are some options to help keep the costs in check.

1. Use a Deejay

A deejay is almost always less expensive than a band, since there are fewer artists and less equipment to cover.

2. Think Outside the Box

Check at music academies and universities to find talented students who can work your wedding, get valuable professional experience, and charge far less than wedding musicians. Just audition them well first. Some couples find talented musicians at bookstores and coffee shops, too.

3. Go All-Inclusive

Hire a group that brings all of their own supplies, not one that requires you to rent tables and a power source for them.

4. DIY!

At a smaller wedding party, or a pre-wedding party, create your own entertainment with your iPod playlists, creating different collections of music to suit the mood of the party, such as soft jazz for the dinner hour and more upbeat songs for dancing.

5. Combine Live and Deejay

If you like the sound of a live performance, ask about an entertainment company's mixed package of a deejay who plays for three hours and a singer who steps in and sings for an hour. It's the best of both worlds.

FLOWERS

Whether you're planning an elaborate floral scheme or a simple one, these tips can help save you money.

1. Buy Local

Use in-season, locally available flowers, which are priced lower than imported flowers.

2. Think Small

Choose smaller bouquets and centerpieces that require fewer flowers. Use just a few exotic flowers in your pieces for visual impact, rather than designing big collections of cheap flowers like carnations. Consider single-stem "bouquets" such as calla lilies or roses instead of full, round bridal bouquets and spend one-tenth the money.

3. Think Simple

Remember that it's the labor that costs the most, so choose hand-tied bouquets that are simpler and less time-consuming for a florist to make.

4. DIY

Take a DIY bouquet-assembly class at the local craft store so that you can make your own easy, hand-tied bouquets together with crafty bridesmaids or relatives, getting your flowers from a trusted source such as Whole Foods or even at discount from

Costco. If you're not the DIY type, ask a talented friend to make these as her wedding gift to you.

5. Emphasize Color, Not Size

Use single, pretty flowers such as elegant calla lilies or bright Gerber daisies—three for you, and one each for your brides-maids—tied with a satin ribbon for an easy, inexpensive and unique bouquet alternative.

DÉCOR

These ideas will help you avoid busting your budget on over-the-top decorations.

1. Emphasize the Site's Attributes

Less is more. Go for simple elegance rather than over-the-top. Use the *site's* beauty, such as windows that overlook the beach or mountains, beautiful gardens, lit up trees. You might not need much décor other than the view.

2. Borrow from the Site

Ask what the site has on hand for you to borrow. Many sites keep a collection of candelabras, pedestals and other décor items you won't have to rent from an outside agency.

3. Shop at Craft Stores

Get plenty of candles and vases from a craft shop where bulk pricing might net you great décor items for less than a dollar each.

4. Don't Overdo It

Don't think that you have to decorate every table, such as the cake table, the family photo table, or the gift table. A simple bud vase with one rose is ideal for the guest book table, for instance. Perhaps you love the look of a single flower lying on the table, rather than standing solo in a vase? Arrange for that to be your theme floral décor at each table.

5. Use the Architecture

If the site has beautiful doors or fireplaces with dramatic mantels, ask if you can place small floral pieces on each to bring the eye to existing, impressive features of the room.

INVITATIONS

With the advent of invitation companies online in addition to the traditional print offerings, you can easily find an elegant option that won't cost a fortune.

1. Choose a Smaller Size

Choose smaller, less ornate invitations rather than an oversized designer style that costs twice as much.

2. Keep Fonts in Check

Use one to two fonts, rather than paying extra for multiple print styles as offered by a professional printer or invitation company. If you're a classic bride, you will likely appreciate the formal look of just one type of font for a unified look, while more artistic brides planning informal weddings tend to choose two different fonts.

3. Don't Upgrade the Paper

Choose classic papers for your invitations, not pricey vellum alternatives.

4. Print Them Yourself

Invest in invitation-making software like Printing Press from *www.mountaincow.com* and create your own invitations and print items using papers from the craft store or office supply store. Or, skip the software and create your own using your computer's word processing software. Since printer ink is expensive and can some-times create rippled pages from ink saturation on larger graphics, you may be better off taking one invitation to a copy shop for a budget-priced printing job.

5. Don't Order More Than You Need

Order the correct amount of invitations after taking a very close look at your final headcount. It's good to have 10 percent extra in case of envelope wording mistakes and also for keepsakes, but you don't want to pay for a hundred more than you need.

PHOTOGRAPHY

Of course, you need pictures of the big day! But with some packages costing up to several thousand dollars, many people need some ways to bring down the cost.

1. Don't Have the Photographer There the Entire Time

Choose the budget package, which might allow for fewer hours of the photographer's time, and capture pre-wedding images with your own digital camera instead of having a pro there charging by the hour. It might not be your style to have a photographer fol-lowing you around all day anyway. After a few hours of that, you might be happy to be left alone to enjoy your party, posing for candids taken by guests.

2. Order a Logical Number of Proofs

Choose the right amount of print proofs. You won't need more than 300. Most couples say the 500 they ordered made it *very* difficult to choose thirty images for their albums.

3. Get Free Proofs

Choose a photographer who provides free print proofs, rather than images online only. While some professional photographers only offer contact sheets or proofs with their logos stamped on them, others still provide the real deal as part of even budget packages. Ask about this when interviewing photographers. If yours provides free print proofs to keep, this gives you a nice supply of free pictures with which to build albums for your parents, bridal party, and yourselves.

4. Select a Standard Album

Choose a basic album, not a leather-bound edition with engravings and other extras. It might not be your plan to display your wedding album in your home, so the ultra-formal leather album might not be a necessity. You can always create a more formal, leather-bound album later, such as an anniversary gift for your spouse years from now. For gift albums such as those for the bridal party and parents of the child attendants, you can order them inexpensively online at Kodak Gallery, Snapfish, and Shutterfly, using the many digital photos taken at the wedding by your friends and family.

5. Stick with One Pro

Hire just the one photographer for your day. A good pro will capture images from all angles.

VIDEOGRAPHY

While photos are a great keepsake, some couples also want the live footage to watch, so they don't miss anything!

1. Limit the Time You Pay For

Choose the budget package for fewer hours of coverage, and capture your own pre-wedding images with your own camera.

2. Hire Only One Person

Skip the three-camera-angles option, which many experts offer for "better editing." You only need one quality professional to capture all the action.

3. Say No to Special Effects

Skip the special effects, such as fading from color to black and white or strobe-type effects. A simple capturing of the day is all that's needed.

4. Get Free Copies

Negotiate for extra copies of the video to give to parents. Many pros will throw in two free copies for you.

5. Buy Raw Footage

Order the raw footage of your wedding, which you will be handed on a mini disk. You can have it professionally edited, or do it yourself, later. When you retain your master version of your wedding video and edit it yourself later, you get to create a far more customized version including the footage *you* really want—such as your parents dancing—rather than what the videographer thought was important to include in a final edit, such as just you dancing.

TRANSPORTATION

You need to get to the wedding somehow, right? Here are some ways to arrive in style with money to spare.

1. Price-Check Different Options

Get a regular limo instead of a stretch limo to save hundreds of dollars. Ask if a black limo costs less than a white limo.

2. Use Your Own Car

Use your own car, which you can decorate with signs, flowers, and other décor—which you can't do with a limo these days.

3. Rent a Classic Car

Check with local classic car clubs to see if any members rent out their cars for weddings at prices way less than limo companies. If you have a favorite classic car, such as a Rolls Royce or Aston Martin, you could bring this special, personalized touch into your day for far less than trying to book a classic car through a limo company.

4. Consider Your Travel Time

Keep timing in mind. Limo companies will charge you from the minute the car leaves the lot until it returns back to base. If your sites are far apart, you could be paying a lot in traveling time.

5. Limit the Number of People in Limos

If your budget is tight, consider asking a family member or friend with a comfortable, clean car to chauffer some members of the wedding party or honored guests. Another option is using the free shuttle bus offered by your guests' hotel to bring everyone to and from the ceremony and reception sites, then back to the hotel at the end of the night. When you book hotel room blocks, this free shuttle service is often included if you ask for it, and guests love the "party bus" mood of traveling with friends to the after-party.

WEDDING GOWN

Brides quickly learn the range of prices for wedding gowns. Following are some ideas to find something that suits your style and your budget.

1. Visit Sample and Trunk Sales

Get on mailing lists for dress shops' sample and trunk sales to get over 50 percent off dresses and accessories that are clearing out to make room for the new season's designs.

2. Shop at Big Stores

Shop at department stores, especially during sales, to earn big discounts on formal dresses and prom dresses that may be white and bridal-appropriate, or the nonbridal, colored style you desire. Department stores such as Macy's, Lord & Taylor, Bloomingdales, and even Neiman Marcus are also great sources of formal event dresses and gowns that may work beautifully as your wedding gown. They may offer seasonal sales of up to 60 percent off to make room for incoming designs.

3. Check out a "Regular" Clothing Store

Visit your favorite dress shops like Ann Taylor to look at their Celebrations lines of formal dresses and shoes. And don't forget J. Crew's lovely line of destination wedding gowns at budget prices, also often included in attractive storewide seasonal sales.

4. Consider a White Bridesmaid Dress

Shop from the bridesmaid dress rack. That hot pink gown might come in white or off-white, or another color you want, for a price of just $100. The poofy, traditional bridal gown might not be your style at all. You may decide that the stylish strapless bridesmaid dress is the perfect choice for you, and you'll be thrilled to pay a *tenth* of the cost!

5. Check Out Alternative Stores

Scope out the locations of outlet stores and outlet shopping centers featuring over twenty designer-name stores. Use *www .outletbound.com* to locate these terrific shopping centers where you might find a designer wedding dress for up to 70 percent off. And visit consignment shops in various neighborhoods as the new, hot source for designer wedding dresses, veils, headpieces, tiaras, and more, at up to 80 percent off. Recent brides often bring their pricey dresses and accessories to these shops to recoup some of their high price tags, and you reap the benefits of the ultra-low prices. If you love heirloom gowns, visit antique stores for beautifully preserved lace dresses in your wished-for Victorian- or 1920s-theme style for big savings as well.

VEIL

Here's how to save money on a very important accessory!

1. Check Out Sample or Trunk Sales

Shop sample or trunk sales for discounts at bridal gown shops.

2. Shop Online

Veils and headpieces are great buys on eBay as other brides unload their investments to recoup their own expenses. You might find a designer style for half the price.

3. Customize What You Find at Local Consignment Shops

Visit consignment shops, especially in the richer areas of town, to find veils and headpieces at a fraction of retail prices, and then use your crafting skills to customize the piece with extra crystals, lace edging, or other additions to make it more *you*. A talented friend or relative can be entrusted with this DIY project as her wedding gift to you.

4. Borrow One

Borrow a relative's or friend's headpiece and/or veil for free.

5. DIY!

Make your own veil using an easy kit from the craft store, or have a crafty friend make your veil for you from scratch. Since the veil is often removed right after the ceremony for easier mingling and dancing, create an inexpensive hair décor look for the rest of the celebration by borrowing a parent's or grandparent's jeweled hair clips, or find these as well at consignment and antique shops for a great "second look" when your veil comes off.

FAVORS

Try these unique favor ideas that are also cost-conscious.

1. Buy in Bulk

Choose candies bought in bulk from a candy shop or warehouse store like Costco, and create small baggies of color-coordinated sweets to hand out as favors. To personalize your favors, use your favorite type of candy, or package up a combination of both your and your groom's favorite candies. For a slightly higher price, you can even order personalized M&Ms in your choice of color combinations, featuring your own wording or pictures on the candies (*www.mms.com*).

2. Check Out Party Stores

Visit party supply stores for fun, kitschy, theme-appropriate favors for less than a dollar each. Party stores stock décor and favor items in many different theme designs, so they might be your best first stop when searching for the perfect, unique, even funny favor items.

3. Bake a Batch!

Edible favors are in, and guests love having their own baggies of chocolate chip cookies, oatmeal cookies, frosted brownies and bars, or even Rice Krispie Treats to munch on during their rides home. When you bake these yourself, the savings add up. Many couples are planning a group baking night to share the task with bridal party members, parents, and even their kids. Wrap each in a baggie or take-home cake box from the craft store, and affix a personalized label you make yourself.

4. Flowering Favors

Shop at your local nursery for tiny, individually potted flowers or herbs as the perfect, living favor that guests can take home and enjoy, or plant in their own gardens for less than $3 apiece in most instances. Packets of flower seeds are also hot favor ideas for just a few dollars each.

5. Make a Donation

Donate to a charity in lieu of favors, but attach a candy to the card announcing that a donation has been made to your favorite cause. The edible gift makes the donation all the sweeter. For instance, you might add a heart-shaped chocolate as a theme-appropriate accent to your announcement that you've donated to the American Heart Association.

CHAPTER 8
DIY Contributions

In keeping with the budget angle, this chapter shows you how to stage various do-it-yourself plans, together with crafty volunteers, to add more meaning to elements of your day. You dream it, you do it . . . and it's yours. Everything from the cake to the centerpieces, your bouquets, and the theme items you'll need are yours to design, craft, and present. Guests will be amazed at the professional-looking results, and don't be surprised if they ask you to create similar pieces for their own family weddings. More than a few brides have turned their own wedding DIY skills into a *business*, preferring the hands-on, creative lifestyle to desk-sitting, spreadsheets, and performance reviews. So I Way DIY plans could potentially lead to you a whole new happier career.

An even bigger perk: DIY projects *really* allow you to have your wedding your way. Think about it. When your local florist creates a round rose bouquet for you, she's probably using the same techniques and flowers she uses in just about every bouquet she makes. Artists have a signature style, and hers may be a certain pattern of floral placement with exactly thirty roses per bouquet and certain filler flowers . . . meaning your bouquet will look very much like those of the brides before and after you, plus or minus a few gardenias or lilies. But when you take on the task of making your own bouquet, *you don't have the experience to make one in a style identical to someone else's.* Whatever you make is *your* signature style. It probably won't look like every other bride's floral piece in town, because you're adding your own flowers in your own choice of dimension and your own spiral pattern, your choice of color shading, your choice of greenery.

> " We *wish* we had designed our own flowers. We asked for all-white flowers for the tribute floral arrangement at our ceremony, and our florist designed an all-*pink* tribute arrangement because she thought it would photograph better against all of the white florals in the room. She just didn't listen to us. " *—Serena,* **newlywed**

The same theory holds true for any and every DIY project you tackle. There has never been another one like it. Which is exactly your aim when designing your wedding your way.

DIY Helps Avoid Surprises

When wedding industry artists take creative license with your plans, that's where you lose your control of the details. And you don't find out about it until you're walking down the aisle or approaching the chafing dishes at your cocktail party. *Who ordered lamb?* These types of wedding surprises may be the work of a mad genius caterer, or it could be the devious work of a parent who just couldn't accept your decision to go all-vegetarian at your wedding. Unbeknownst to you, that parent made a call to the caterer and requested some meat.

While self-catering the entire reception is not very high on most couples' priority lists, or within their capabilities, keep this one in mind for smaller wedding parties like the rehearsal dinner or the morning-after breakfast. DIY catering means you get to keep control over the menu. If a certain type of fare is your big wish for any manageable party, you might find it wiser—and more fun—to gather some friends for a cooking party and whip up batches of your own recipes for the event.

Who's on Your DIY Team?

Sunita brings up a very important element of the DIY approach: you need dedicated volunteers who bring talent and skill to the table. They don't have to have degrees from a culinary arts institute—some wedding projects require little more than printing out labels and sticking them on bottles or CDs. As one bride said while wrist-deep in colored sand from a craft project, "A monkey could do this job."

" At first we were afraid to self-cater our rehearsal dinner, but once we brought in the bridesmaids and the groomsmen, we all had a blast in our kitchen putting together the platters, slicing the vegetables, seasoning and grilling them, all while enjoying a few bottles of wine and terrific together time in the kitchen and out on the terrace. It was a highlight of our pre-wedding preparations. " —*Sunita*, **newlywed**

FIGURE OUT WHAT YOU NEED

So establish the skill levels needed for each DIY project you'd like to share with volunteers. Write down the project and list every skill needed: graphic design, collating, tying ribbon bows, affixing stickers, candymaking, baking, stapling, what have you.

Some crafts require almost no brainpower, while others, like sewing hems or frosting intricately designed wedding cake layers, do require certain skills.

BE UP FRONT WITH YOUR REQUEST

When seeking volunteers for any wedding crafts, make sure your invitation e-mail lets them know exactly what will be involved, *and how much time is needed.* "Join me this Sunday afternoon from 2 P.M. to 4 P.M. for a cupcake-making party. No design experience needed — you'll just be on frosting duty, and décor is stick-in, store-bought sugar butterflies. 200 of them! I need your help, so please join me for wine, cheese, and lots of great conversation as we work on the sweet stuff for the wedding."

With all information clear and direct, you'll have happy volunteers joining you to bring your craft projects to life.

CONSIDER YOUR NETWORK

Another question to ask yourself when it comes to your DIY team is: *who has which skills and connections?* You might know that your sister is a master at sewing projects and could potentially make all of your table runners, plus your aisle runner. It didn't even occur to you to create those things until you remembered her beautiful table runner at the last family Thanksgiving. One call to her and you could save thousands of dollars *and* have creative control over the design and fabrics. Your brother-in-law might have a friend who works for a theater company. Could he handle the lighting effects for your reception or hook you up with an artist who creates set decorations? When you start looking at your circles of loved ones in terms of who they know and what they can do, you can find additional options for designing your wedding your way.

INCLUDE THE KIDS!

Don't forget that *kids* are essential parts of your wedding team, especially since most of them are way more adept with computer technology than you are. Your twelve-year-old niece might be able to edit a slideshow of your baby pictures in twenty minutes flat, and if she has aspirations to be a filmmaker someday, this is a fine experience for her—and a first professional credit! Your fifteen-year-old stepbrother could add moving caricatures of you to your personal wedding website. The flower girls can definitely scoop M&Ms into favor bags alongside you as you all work on crafts for the centerpieces. Do you have kids who bring skills to the table?

WHO DO YOU KNOW? Ask your groom, parents, family, and friends if they know anyone with special talents or skills that can help with your wedding plans. This brainstorming session could reveal a winning option.

Let's Be Realistic

Before you create a long list of DIY projects that includes everything from making all of your centerpieces and building a chuppah from scratch to baking your wedding cake and making your dress, you have to face some reality. These tasks are *important*, and you'll need to be able to devote enough time to each of them. Don't assume that each can be done in a day, or that a craft you see outlined online is as easy as it looks. You may need to block off triple the time you think a craft will take in order to allow you a calm pace, plus the time for a do-over if you mess up.

> **"** We asked my friend to create the cover designs for our DIY invitations and sent her the file with the wording and layout we wanted. When she showed up with the finished project, the cover graphic was in black and white with shades of gray, not the orange we asked for. At first, we were upset, but then once we looked at it some more, the black, white, and gray gave our invitations a very elegant look and coordinated beautifully with the black print of the invitation wording inside. Her unintentional design turned it into something way better than what we originally wanted." —*Hayley*, newlywed

Also, accept that you don't have the years of experience or the professional training that a wedding vendor has. These pros know which flowers open up perfectly when popped into a tub of warm water seventeen minutes before the ceremony, and which will wilt when the temperature hits seventy-nine degrees Fahrenheit. If you decide to take on a pro's job, you accept the risks that you may make beginner's mistakes and that your choices and handiwork may not produce absolutely perfect results. Are you willing to take on that risk? Your volunteers, too, may not be experts, so you'll have to accept a font that's not the one you envisioned when Aunt Ida arrives with the two hundred programs she's printed up, beaming with joy that she made such beautiful pieces for you. This is not the time to be Tyrant Bride, sending your Aunt Ida home in tears with instructions to redo the entire batch in Arial font. Yes, it's your wedding your way, but don't get insane about these tiny details. When you have DIY projects, and when you delegate DIY projects, reality may create a slightly different form than you expected. Which can produce charm rather than catastrophe.

Any DIY maven has to be flexible, and to have trust.

Just the Right Resources

You're using good resources to plan your wedding as a whole—a good book like this one, bridal magazines, referrals from trusted friends and vendors—so the same rule applies to your DIY contributions to your dream wedding. You'll have much more success, and enjoy the process more, if you have clear directions in front of you, the best materials, and information that gives you *confidence* to create one-of-a-kind, gorgeous elements for your day.

Here are the top resources you need to consult for any DIY projects you have in mind:

- **A trusted online source for crafts.** It might be Martha Stewart's site *(www.marthastewart.com)* where crafts are shown and explained step-by-step, or *Better Homes and Gardens (www.bhg.com)* for their gardening tips, Food Network's recipes *(www.foodtv.com)*, or other favorite sites.
- **Craft store classes.** Check at your local craft store to find out if and when they offer expert-led classes in flower arranging and other crafts. Many classes are free, plus the expense of materials, and you'll get an instant education on hand-tied bouquets, centerpieces, wreaths, garlands, embossing, and other crafts.
- **Florist classes.** Some florists make a little extra money by offering classes in bouquet-, centerpiece-, corsage-, and boutonniere making. Sign up solo or with a few friends so that you all get the skills you need to make your wedding-day florals.
- **Adult school courses.** Many communities offer adult classes in everything from gardening to crafts to dancing, all for low prices and convenient night or weekend scheduling.
- **Cultural associations, which you can find online.** These groups or clubs revolve around certain heritages and their histories, celebrations, and authentic fare. These groups are a goldmine of information,

classes, sometimes free or low-cost rentals of items, and referrals to nearby experts who can give private lessons to your group on the correct way to prepare cultural dishes, drinks, décor, and other items.

- **Craft kits.** Look in your craft store for invitation, veil, décor, and other DIY kits that have fantastic, photo-oriented instructions you can easily follow. Don't limit yourself to the bridal section, though. The photo aisle, the food aisle, and the floral aisle will all have kits you can use.
- **Experienced crafter friends and relatives.** Use the bounty of *their* knowledge and experience to lead your group. You don't always have to be in charge of every task. Let Aunt Ida teach you all about proper print-item creation or favor-making.

The Top Tasks

You may think you know all the usuals—those wedding tasks that everyone and their mother (literally!) decide to craft instead of hire vendors to create. But here's a list of some wedding tasks you might not have thought of, to give you a little bit more inspiration.

FLOWERS
- The basics: bouquets and centerpieces
- Pew or aisle markers
- Floral wreaths for the flower girls' hair accessories
- Tiny flower hairpins
- Fresh flowers to pin onto the back of your dress where the train begins
- Floating single flowers as centerpieces and table accents such as coffee tables in front of fireplaces and other sitting areas
- Floating single flowers for the restrooms (Think a glass bowl filled with water and a gardenia floating on top)

- Floral pieces set on mantels and windowsills
- Flowers attached to green garlands wrapped around banisters and handrails
- Floating flowers set in ponds and pools
- Single flowers set next to platters on the buffet table
- Single flowers pressed into the cake as cake décor
- Single flowers in pretty bud vases placed near the guest book and on the family photo table
- Single flowers, stem-wrapped for presentation as take-home favors
- Flower petals lined up on either side of the aisle, instead of using an aisle runner
- Potted flowers lined up on either side of the aisle, instead of using an aisle runner

DÉCOR
- Ribbon bows for pew or row markers
- Fabric chair covers for the ceremony chairs
- Light strings (think little white holiday lights from your Christmas tree) hung in the trees, on the outline of the tent, in shrubbery and bushes and on mantel garlands.

PRINT ITEMS
- Invitations and save-the-date cards
- Inserts such as response cards and reception cards
- Menu cards
- Place cards
- Table number or name cards
- Maps and driving directions
- Signage at your ceremony and reception sites, giving guests directions on where to go

- Framed 3" × 5" cards explaining who is in each family photo on display
- Printed "wish cards" on which guests write their wishes for you, and then insert in a silver or glass bowl

CAKE AND DESSERTS

- Wedding cake
- Groom's cake
- Cupcake platter in place of a cake, or in addition to the cake
- Dessert bar items such as pies, tartlets, brownies, cookies, mousses, and other specialties
- Chocolate-dipped fruits
- Fresh fruit platter, with fruits cut into creative shapes
- Ice cream bar, with lots of fun toppings including sprinkles, caramel sauce, whipped cream, cherries, walnuts, and more

FOOD AND DRINKS

- For pre-wedding parties, post-wedding parties and *small* weddings only, since you don't want to take on too much—appetizers, family-style platters, slow-cooker recipes like pulled pork to serve on small dishes
- Bite-sized foods such as sliders, canapés, goat cheese mini pizza rounds, fresh shrimp on skewers with pineapple, fresh vegetable platters, grilled vegetable platters, meatballs on toothpicks
- Family-favorite recipes such as bean dips and spinach quiches
- Fruit platters, especially with tropical fruits cut into creative shapes
- Sangrias or punches, with or without alcohol
- Mixed drinks such as pomegranate martinis
- Gourmet water garnishes, such as skewers of fruits or lemon and lime slices

GOWN AND ACCESSORIES

- Wedding gown creation, using a skilled dressmaker working off of a photo or pattern
- Alterations to an heirloom gown, such as removing sleeves and adding a train
- Alterations to a used gown bought on eBay
- Veil creation
- Accents added to a veil, such as gluing on Swarovski crystals or lace appliqués
- Accents to a hat or headband, such as attaching fresh flowers
- Sewing accents to elbow-length gloves, such as silver-embroidered monogramming
- Sewing accents to a plain train, such as lace appliqués or embroidery

WHAT ABOUT PHOTOGRAPHY, VIDEOGRAPHY, AND ENTERTAINMENT? Most couples want to leave these tasks to the pros, since they are such a big part of the wedding day, and self-done efforts in these arenas often leave couples disappointed when a cousin misses important shots during the ceremony, or a friend who promised to play the guitar during the cocktail party has had a few too many drinks. Photos, video, and entertainment are great DIY options for pre- and post-wedding parties, of course, but steer clear of trying to assign too many important tasks to friends. You don't want important guests *working* on your wedding day.

TRANSPORTATION

- Decorating your own car using nontoxic temporary paint pens to read "Going to the Chapel" or your names and wedding date on the windows
- Affixing wedding-themed magnetic signs

- Displaying a Just Married sign in the back window (but not blocking your view while driving)
- Floral garlands to lay on an open convertible

PHOTOGRAPHY

- After the wedding, you can make DIY wedding albums and scrapbooks, for your own keepsakes and as gifts to others, putting your own personal touches and statements into them without paying a fortune for professional albums that limit the amount of personalization you can do. Many pro albums limit you to black or ivory pages with black or ivory mats, and your DIY albums might have brighter mats and multiple images per page, digitally added captions, and space for attaching your wedding invitation and other fun items.

- Go to *www.kodakgallery.com, www.snapfish.com,* or *www.shutterfly .com* to learn how easy it is to create your own wedding albums from your digital photos, or you can just slide those free proofs into store-bought photo albums in fun colors. This is one area where a DIY plan allows you far more personalization at a far more comfortable price if your one main photo album is included in the price of your photography package and additional albums cost hundreds of dollars.

> " Our package allowed for two professional albums, which we ordered for our parents since they're ultra-traditional and would like the black mats and other standard features. We preferred to have a green album with sage green pages, so we made our own wedding album, which looks far better on display in our living room than that standard photo album ever would. " —*Lila,* newlywed

Where can you put a personal twist on a traditional item? Which DIY projects have sparked your imagination? And can you *imagine* how much fun it will be to work with friends and relatives on your collection of creative tasks? For many couples, it's the *process* of working with their friends on DIY projects, spending quality and laugh-filled time together, that becomes a highlight of their wedding planning season.

Part Four

GETTING MORE TIME WITH GUESTS

This section shares the top ideas for planning the ideal wedding weekend events that allow you to spend quality time with your guests, not work your butt off at yet another big event. The wedding weekend is time to kick back and relax, not slave over a stove. So every chapter here has a focus on keeping work to a minimum and socializing to a maximum, with sentimental and fun activities blended into food plans, décor, invitation, and etiquette tips.

CHAPTER 9

Pre-Wedding

When your wedding weekend *finally* arrives, it may seem like years since you first started planning, or it might seem like weeks. The process may have been laborious and stressful, depending on how many clashes you experienced with parents, vendors, and bridal party members, or it may have been a breeze. (I'm hoping it was a breeze!) Whatever the hills and valleys of your path to this point, this is *the fun part*. You're moving out of planning mode, where every detail is on paper or in your mind, into reality mode, when your ideas start to come to life in full color, texture, scent, and taste.

Add in the delicious fact that this is when *friends and family* start arriving, thereby adding the heartfelt element of togetherness to your wedding celebration, and you'll be over the moon with your hard (yet enjoyable) planning work coming to fruition. Finally!

A Few Last-Minute Tips

It's entirely true that the days immediately before the wedding can make or break the success of your big day. Plenty of experts are busily assembling your orders, putting the finishing touches on your design elements. Your own inner circle of bridal party members and family members may also be working on the tasks they have taken on. *You* have your own list of things to do as well, not the least of which is confirming progress and completion with every single member of your team. In this section, you'll take a deep breath and work through the last-minute essentials, always ready to save the day with an innovative solution for an unforeseen snafu. It happens in just about every wedding that something cannot go as planned. What's the key to success? Keeping your cool, staying organized, and knowing that you can handle everything beautifully.

- It's very likely that you won't have *all* of your pre-wedding tasks completed by the big day—after all, some things can only be done the day before. So, block off a few hours of the *morning* on the day before the wedding and dedicate them to running your errands or working on DIY projects. If you leave tasks to the afternoon or evening, you run the risk of either being late or being too exhausted to focus well on planning tasks, not to mention the disappointment of having to leave the first festive gathering to go iron thirty tablecloths at home. Completing your tasks in the morning releases you from stress, gives you that wonderful "Done!" feeling and lets you move forward with greeting your arriving guests and getting the celebration started.

- Arrange ahead of time to be granted cell phone access to all of your wedding vendors. Some coordinators open their cell lines up to wedding couples only within the forty-eight-hour window of the approaching wedding—prior to that, you left messages or sent e-mails like all of their other clients. It's a wise move to switch to *your* best timeframes by asking your vendors to allow you morning or evening access to them via cell phone or text.

- Consider hiring a wedding coordinator to handle all of the last-minute tasks and scrambling, which would have them taking over on the day before the wedding, fielding all of the phone calls from your deejay and photographer, reminding vendors of directions and itineraries, tracking down missing deliveries of flowers and rental items, and so on. Then you can relax and enjoy your arriving guests, knowing that the legwork of your wedding plans is being handled by a pro. Visit *www.bridalassn.com* to find a coordinator near you, and explore your prospective candidates' day-of wedding packages. You do have the power to custom-create plans with most coordinators today, such as hiring them for three-day help as opposed to just running the show on the wedding day itself. Some brides want full access for the entire month before the wedding, and that can be arranged. Concerned about the cost? Most couples say every penny was worth it for the peace of mind they and their families experienced. No one's mother was crying about a wrinkled dress, no one's siblings were up all night fixing the buckling dance floor the rental agency shoddily laid in the backyard, and no one missed a day-before party because they had to drive all over town looking for enough matching taper candles.

- Give yourselves some downtime *before* your social downtime. This means putting the clipboard and cell phone away and going for a walk together, or playing some basketball out on the driveway, or just cuddling up on the couch to share some quiet time alone. Even if it's just twenty minutes, it'll fortify you for the days ahead.

- Stash the dress and accessories. If you'll host a rehearsal dinner at your place the night before the wedding, or if guests are likely to drop by your house, make sure your gown and accessories are safely tucked away in a locked bedroom where they can sit out unseen by your groom, out of reach of guests, and far from any sources of stains or other dangers. That locked bedroom door—make sure you have the key before you close it!—keeps your most important wedding preparations safe and at the ready, completely organized and out of the crushing plastic garment bag. Just fluff and hang, and then close that door.

- Create your must-have bag, including the marriage license, wedding rings, and other essentials, and store them someplace safe and in view—perhaps right next to your dress—so that they don't get left behind on the wedding day.

WAIT, WASN'T MORNING THE PLAN? The reason I recommend getting evening access to your vendors is that some don't have business hours until 10 A.M. or 11 A.M., so your early-bird task timing isn't optimal for reaching them. But if you can connect with your vendors via phone the night *before*, your vendors have time to research what you need, make some calls, arrange for first-thing delivery, and grant your wishes for your *morning* working time.

With these smart steps in place, you're ready to join the celebrations!

Arrival Day Cocktails and Open House Party

Too many brides and grooms miss out on this opportunity to visit and have fun with their guests, since they assume they're going to be too busy the day before the wedding. Hey, if they don't organize their timing, they *will* be too busy! You're going to be far more efficient, since greeting your guests upon their arrival *is* a top priority of yours. Sure, they could be left to check into their hotel and run into each other in the hallways or down at the pool, but it's far more exciting for them—and for you—if you plan a special welcome for them. With you both in attendance.

PARTIES AT THE HOTEL

Consider planning a welcome cocktail party for the afternoon of guests' arrival, coordinated with the check-in times (usually 3 P.M. to 4 P.M.). Plan with your hotel manager to set up a buffet of light hors d'oeuvres, cheese platter, fruits, and drinks in the hotel atrium. When guests arrive, they'll be given their welcome baskets and told that you're waiting for them out at the cocktail party. Or, you can set up an open-house style cocktail party in one of the hotel rooms, perhaps the suite you've booked for the bridal party or even for yourselves. Three or four party platters, wine and beer, and a collection of glasses can be set on the desk and dressers. Guests can pop in for a visit or stay as long as they'd like. Some hotel rooms on the ground floor open out to terraces and lawn expanses, so you may wish to guide your guests out into the sunshine and lounge chairs for an outdoor party.

" Our hotel manager gave us 50 percent discounts off of our welcome party *and* our rehearsal dinner because we booked over twenty rooms in our room block. When we told him we wanted to host our after-party there as well, he gave us two big food platters for free. " —*Ashley,* **newlywed**

What about just having everyone gather at the hotel bar? That can turn into a big bar tab, so if that's your plan, arrange with the hotel manager for a preplanned menu with a selection of bar food platters and *x* number of wine bottles or drinks brought to your tables. While some couples don't worry about expense, most prefer to keep this party under a certain dollar amount, so they arrange for a set menu of options for their guests. Keep in mind that this welcome cocktail party has quickly become a sought-after event for *parents* to host, especially if they didn't get to host an engagement party, or if you're paying for the majority of your wedding. Either set of parents, or both sets, might take on the expense of this soiree, welcoming both sides of the family and your friends in fine style.

A key to the welcome cocktail party is keeping it easily accessible. With guests driving five or six hours just to get to the hotel sometimes, they'd rather relax and socialize right there instead of driving another half hour to your parents' house. This makes the hotel-based welcome party the top location option. You're looking out for your guests' comfort level, and—let's face it—you're also keeping the party out of your home, which might already be cleaned and prepped for tomorrow morning's pre-ceremony breakfast. Hosting more than one event at your home is usually a *lot* to undertake, with setup and cleanup threatening to exhaust you. Instead, stick to the attractions and amenities of the hotel. A poolside cocktail party is a top trend, and hotel catering managers often hand along terrific discounts to wedding groups for these welcome gatherings. You may be able to get two hours of open bar and up to six food platters for 50 to 60 percent off their regular catering prices. They're just glad to have your guests, and perhaps your wedding, booked at their hotel.

WELCOME PARTIES AT HOME

If the hotel doesn't offer much in the way of atriums, poolside party areas, or a nice bar or lounge, you might decide that an at-home welcome party is the way to go. "We bought our house six months before the wedding, we've worked hard to fix it up, and we really wanted to invite our out-of-town friends and family to come see it. We had it catered, and everyone enjoyed the 'comforts of home,' such as sitting out on our deck or watching television in our basement den. This was our first big party at our place, and it was fantastic," say Elizabeth and Devon, who say they spent just $150 on party platters and drinks for their thirty guests. They also say that having plenty of comfy couches was a big reason they chose their home over a hotel suite as their party location. "We knew guests would want to kick back and relax after long flights or drives."

Parents can also host welcome cocktail parties, perhaps with their own guests invited to their own homes, which allows you to host your friends at the hotel or at your place. There's no rule saying only one person can host a welcome gathering. The scattered-parties approach allows more people to have the joy of sharing their home, and it means they will not have to provide food and drink for so many guests. So if you have a long list of out-of-town guests, consider letting parents know about this option. They'd get to host their parties their way and perhaps use some of the ideas they originally suggested for the wedding at their own events. Everybody wins, and you get to spend more quality time with your friends on your own time and terms, which may be a big draw for you.

Let all hosts know about the open house arrangement, to accommodate guests who might arrive in the morning, as well as those who arrive in the afternoon. The party is ongoing, guests come and go as they please, and the party is closed down well before any planned rehearsal dinner, allowing everyone the time to get showered and ready for the next event on your agenda.

Rehearsal Dinner

For many years, this party has been the traditional domain of the groom's parents, while the bride's parents were deeply involved with planning and paying for the wedding. Times have, obviously, changed. Now, it's *you* planning your wedding, and your parents may be helping plan and pay for different *parts* of the wedding plan, in your own custom arrangement.

WHO HOSTS IT?

You might have many options for who will host the rehearsal dinner. If you're among the couples who took on the entire wedding plans, including paying for it, you might have decided to give the rehearsal dinner to your groom's parents to plan, while your parents get the morning-after breakfast. That's the going trend right now, as couples understand their parents' wishes to enjoy planning *something*.

Are couples giving the rehearsal dinner to *both* sets of parents? Some are, in cases where both sets of parents have known each other for a long time, get along well, work together well, and perhaps co-planned an engagement party or shower for you. If they've shown they can share the reins, you might decide to let them partner on this party. If they're virtual strangers, or if you fear they'd battle for superiority or clash over guest lists, menus, and budgets, you're best off dividing the parties.

HOW ARE YOU INVOLVED?

Let's assume your groom's parents are hosting the rehearsal dinner. What kind of creative control can you expect? That all depends on how they feel about your ownership of the wedding itself. If they're the least bit bitter about that, they may clasp this party to their bosom and not let you near. They may counter your requests with a sour, immature, "you have your own event planned, now leave us alone to plan ours." It's happened many times before. Do you just give up and let them plan their party, their way? Or do you fight them on the plans that you've granted them permission to make?

You all have to meet in the middle. Look back at Chapter 5 on the care and handling of parents as a reminder of the best way to remain in control of your wedding weekend events while still giving parents the best dose of satisfaction. It would be a grave mistake to forget your already-honed skills, surrendering to a bossy parent's guilt trip and settling for a rehearsal dinner that *competes with* or *outshines* the wedding. Yes, some parents actually aim to knock the rehearsal dinner out of the park, pouring money into it, going overly indulgent as a way to show off to the guests, and stealing the bride and groom's wedding-day thunder. You couldn't afford lobster tails? They have entire lobsters on the menu. You couldn't afford champagne? They have *magnums* of it. "But we're doing this for *you!*" is what most parents say when confronted by the irate wedding couple, and that statement is usually true. Most parents aren't diabolical. Most parents don't try to outshine their adult children's wedding plans. They're just trying to plan a lavish event, and include the details they would have included in the reception menu, if they had been asked. Why on earth would you be offended about lobster tails and magnums of champagne? It's not like that makes your chicken and pasta entrées look . . . oh. Most parents truly don't understand until hindsight smacks them in the head that their one-upping the reception plans is a horrendous mistake.

So when you grant the rehearsal dinner to a set of parents, clarify at the start that you have a few firm rules about what fits best with the wedding weekend plans as a whole. "The location is up to you, the guest list is up to you, and the time of night is up to you, but we *strongly* request that you plan a family-style, Italian sit-down dinner rather than the same type of buffet all the guests are getting the next day. We want it to be as different from the wedding as possible, so that our guests get variety and the chance to enjoy the great Italian food we have around here."

You have to make it clear what you prefer *way* in advance. Some parents book rehearsal dinners nine months ahead of time, and you don't want to be told "We set our menu already, so you're going to have to arrange the cocktail party and dinner menu items around *our* choices." *We got to it first* is not the most mature attitude, but it is one way that some parents try to balance their loss of control over the wedding. If parents say they placed an order, just come back with, "Well, they didn't order the shrimp cocktail and lobster already, so there's plenty of time to make a change to the menu. I really think everyone is going to be thrilled to taste the local cuisine."

" My parents became very overwhelmed very quickly about the rehearsal dinner, since friends of theirs told them they had to invite *all* the out-of-town guests. That would have put the guest count for the rehearsal dinner at more than 100 people. We had to tell my parents to stop listening to their friends' advice or stories about what they did, forget about competing with anyone else, and just ask *us* if they have any questions. We told them it was fine etiquette-wise to invite just the bridal party, their guests and the officiant, and the guest list was back down to twenty-five. Problem solved. " —*Sarah*, newlywed

As you know, all turn-downs are to be delivered with sweetness and sincerity. Parental hosts may need a guiding hand and perhaps a slight change of direction. If they're concerned about their budget, since your families and bridal party members, and their guests will attend, join in to help devise a budget-friendly yet fun plan. "Your backyard is such a great setting. How about we plan for a gourmet barbecue, with turkey burgers and kebabs, something just a bit different than the usual cookout? Maybe a Greek salad instead of potato salad? Why don't we go to the gourmet market this weekend and do a little bit of scouting?" You're not taking over the plans, but you are keeping your hand in them.

REHEARSAL DINNER THEMES
What are the top trends in rehearsal dinner themes?

* The sit-down dinner at a restaurant still leads the way, followed by sit-down meals at home for a smaller guest list.
* An at-home cocktail party with catered platters and chafing dishes.
* A backyard barbecue with either the old-fashioned standards of hot dogs and hamburgers or gourmet options of kebabs, grilled portabella mushroom caps, and so on.
* Fiesta-style parties are also popular, with sizzling fajita platters served family-style, or build-your-own-burrito bars next to the margarita bar.
* Since all things East-West are perennial favorites at pre-wedding parties, think about creating stations for fried rice, noodles, stir-fry beef or chicken in big woks, spring rolls, and other crowd-pleasers.

The menu often determines the theme, and the vast majority of couples like to choose menu items that didn't make the cut for their wedding menus. If the reception hall's price for a sushi station was astronomical, you can get a sushi platter from Costco for a fraction of the price, and as you're feeding far fewer people, you really get to indulge them.

Don't forget that do-it-yourself options are also a big part of at-home rehearsal dinners. Ask volunteers to help you make stuffed shells or gumbo or chili, whatever their specialty is. Bridal party members might agree to bring a platter of their famous brownies for dessert, and grandparents might whip up a batch of their chocolate mousse. Again, with a small guest list you have greater options, and greater ease of preparation, with DIY meal-planning. And one trip to the discount liquor store will stock you with beers and wines to suit your party's theme. There's no need to stock an entire open bar with every kind of top-shelf liquor known to mankind. You're the hosts, so you can plan a bar with only three or four choices of liquor drinks, plus a variety of soft drinks, iced teas, and sodas.

> " It had been ages since I'd ever attended a party where punch was served, and we couldn't get over how fantastic my mother's peach and champagne infused punch was! Our guests were flipping out over it, and she happily made several batches. " — *Cara*, **newlywed**

One trend for rehearsal dinners is bringing in your sentimental choice of wines, such as the vintage you were drinking when you got engaged. You can share the story with your guests as they enjoy it too. Another option is to order wines that "give back," so visit *www.charitywines.com* to order bottles that benefit different charities. At my own wedding, we ordered several bottles to benefit the Dan Marino Foundation, since my husband is a big Miami Dolphins fan. The site showcases vintages from many different athletes and entertainers, so check to see who's been added lately.

ENTERTAINMENT

Use your iPod for your entertainment needs, interrupting only for the toasts you'll make to your guests for attending, your bridal party for being such an important part of your lives, and your parents for a lifetime of love and support. Etiquette states that the hosts are the first to propose a toast, so let your parents go first if this is their party. It would be a major faux pas for you to clink your knife against your glass to get everyone's attention for a toast when you're not the hosts, so be sure to let parents know that they're welcome to propose the first toast of the evening. (They might not be aware that tradition holds for them to speak first.)

Keep toasts short, then present your bridal party with their gifts, and here's an important moment you shouldn't miss—take your parents aside and thank them personally and privately for their part in helping you make your wedding dreams come true. No matter how large or small a part they played, and especially if they showed great character in allowing you to make your own decisions with their financial contributions. That's a tough thing for parents to do, especially if they've always felt the need to run the show or advise you about how you ought to live your life. If you see that they really accepted that this is your time, that deserves a private thank-you, a hug, and probably some tears of gratitude and joy.

The Wedding Morning (Breakfast and Salon Trip)

This morning is the quiet before the action of the day, when you wake up and blink a few times, realizing, "This is my wedding day." Having an hour of solitude before everything snaps into high gear—with the doorbell ringing and bridesmaids arriving with their dresses, flower girls running around, and a photographer following you—is a brilliant idea. It allows you your first few sips of coffee in peace and quiet, so that a smile can grow across your face, you can look at your gown hanging on the door, and relish your last morning as an unmarried woman.

How did that hectic stuff sound to you? The flurry of visitors, the kids on the scene, the photographer telling you to stop and smile for the camera? Is that the tone you want for your wedding morning? Some brides say yes, and some brides would rather plan for a calmer environment. They're going to be tightly wound enough, they think. They don't want their parents inviting the aunts and uncles over for breakfast, filling your home with even more bodies, more noise, more people asking you if you're really going to wear that shade of pink lipstick.

> " It was a circus at my place on the morning of the wedding! I had originally told my parents that I didn't want a big family breakfast with the grandparents, the aunts and uncles, the child attendants and their parents . . . but my parents said it would be a festive atmosphere. It was nuts! I wish I had stuck to my original plan of just having my bridesmaids over so that we could get our *only* time to ourselves, get ready for the wedding together, and have a champagne toast. That toast never happened because my dad and uncle grabbed the champagne bottle. It's my only wedding regret that I didn't stick to my guns on that one. " —*Debbie*, **newlywed**

SCHEDULING

This is your time to arrange, and the schedule is up to you. The planning factor that might direct your plans is how early your hairstylist and makeup artist will need to arrive at your place. If you only book one hairstylist, as many brides do to save money, she may need to arrive much earlier than you think to have an hour to work on you, then an hour for each of your bridesmaids. So think about your need for quiet time, such as blocking off an hour of solitude before the action starts—you might go for a walk or a jog to clear your mind—then count the number of hours needed and schedule your stylist appropriately. Assume that things will take longer than you think, and leave plenty of time for unforeseen problems.

KEEPING IT SMALL

And what about the parents and the aunts and uncles? You can say "No way," as many brides do these days. They don't want the "festive atmosphere," they don't want to play host, they don't want to make a big breakfast spread for twenty people, and they don't want anyone to see them before they arrive for the ceremony. If that's the case for you, tell your parents, "No, I'd rather be just with my bridesmaids, have breakfast with them and get ready in peace. If I want to walk around in my bra, I'd like to be able to do that. Why don't you have the aunts and uncles over for breakfast at your place?" Many parents love that idea, since they get to plan and host their own morning get-together. Just spell it out.

MAKE SURE YOU EAT! You might be nervous or too excited to eat, but be sure to get some food into your stomach to give you healthy energy, prevent you from getting a hunger headache or passing out, and keep you hydrated. Some brides say their throats were too dry for bread, but they munched on hydrating fruit. Whatever works. And not wanting coffee breath, some stuck with juice. The men need to eat as well, so be sure they have a meal wherever they are. Some brides send over baskets of muffins and bagels or platters of sandwiches to the groom's hotel room, with a private note written to the groom.

INVITING SOME GUESTS

You might be thinking, "But I *want* my parents and grandparents there!" since it would be a fantastic family morning and a great opportunity to take lots of pre-wedding photos once you're dressed up. If you snap the group photos before the ceremony, you'll save time *after* the ceremony and before the cocktail party!

You won't lose those fifteen minutes of gathering your immediate family for group pictures. That's definitely a perk to having them over that morning.

One solution for a crowded house: let the relatives mingle and brunch downstairs while your upstairs level is off-limits. That is where you and your bridesmaids will be getting dressed and enjoying your alone time. You *can* set boundaries to give you the best of both worlds. Send someone downstairs to get your bottle of champagne and a collection of champagne flutes, and there's your girls-only group toast! Other champagne bottles can be served to the visiting relatives downstairs, who you can then join for a second group toast and all the oohs and aahs of admiration when you first step into the room . . . at your perfect timing and on your terms.

FOOD

Whether you have a small gathering or a larger one, you'll likely need to offer some food, with a big focus on ease of preparation and serving. If you're serving breakfast, make regular coffee and decaf, and set out platters of cheese rings, pastries, bagels, muffins, and artisan breads such as whole-grain breads, Asiago cheese breads, and other gourmet flavors. If your wedding takes place in the evening, a lunch may be in order, which could be a "make your own sandwich" bar, with several different types of rolls and breads, slices of turkey and roast beef, grilled vegetables, a salad, and refreshing iced tea or lemonade. Another popular option is the ease of order-in foods such as platters of premade sub sandwiches. Couples on a budget might get cold food party platters from Costco, wanting to avoid the hassle of cooking frozen appetizers or grilling burgers in the yard. Keep foods simple and self-serve for everyone's ease of access and personalized menu choices.

As a general rule, don't serve any foods or garnishes with staining foods such as tomatoes (bruschetta is on the warning list!) or berries, such as blueberry muffins or cherry topping, since those present the risk of damage to your or others' wedding outfits. Just leave them off the menu, and while you're at it, switch from coffee to water once you get your gown on.

> **"**We decorated my maid of honor's minivan with all kinds of signs saying 'Bride on Board' and 'Going to the Chapel,' so the rides to and from the salon were a big celebration as other motorists honked their horns at us and waved, rolled down their windows to wish me luck. The ride was a blast, and we had the best time! **"** —*Hallie*, **newlywed**

You might want to enjoy a meal as a group *before* you and the girls go upstairs to dress, just for comfort's sake and to avoid a mess-the-dress nightmare for anyone before the day even begins. Even with your hair done, your tiara on, and your makeup 90 percent completed, you can have a light meal to keep you energized. Most brides and grooms say they prefer to avoid spicy foods—so chips and salsa might not be on their wish list—if they know they get an upset stomach when stressed.

For additional breakfast ideas, see Chapter 11's section on the morning-after breakfast or brunch. You can incorporate some of the same menu elements.

THE SALON TRIP

If you're not having your hair and makeup done at home, you're probably going to a nearby salon. Some brides invite their mother and mother-in-law to join them, and some bring the flower girls along as well. More and more salons are providing breakfast or lunch spreads and often champagne for their bridal groups, or they might allow you to bring in your own food, which they will set up for you or serve you as you're all in the stylists' chairs. The result is that festive atmosphere you've heard so much about, but it's a controlled atmosphere with professionals working their magic and the kids glowing over their grownup hairdos.

This option may sound way better to you than having everyone clamoring for mirror space in your apartment or house. And having six stylists at your command also means you won't need that 6 A.M. wakeup call for an in-home stylist's solo efforts. Everyone gets their hair and makeup done within an hour or two, and then it's a happy caravan to your house for dressing and photos.

TAKING PHOTOS

Allow for enough time in your wedding-day schedule for your professional photographer to get all those pre-wedding shots. If you're already dressed by the time he arrives, just stage your mom or your maid of honor zipping you up if you want. Then get to the group lineups and duo photos of you with each of your bridesmaids in rapid succession, and think about any silly shots you might want, such as you wearing socks with your wedding gown because you don't want to scuff your wedding shoes, which you're planning to bring with you and slip on right before the ceremony. A good photographer will snap plenty of candids as you and your bridesmaids interact, and these may become far more cherished by you than all those stand-in-a-line pictures.

Watch the clock, since time can whiz by as you're taking photos. You don't want to be late to the ceremony! Know the exact time you all have to depart, and hold firm to it. Even if there are more photos to take. It's okay to say no to a photographer who keeps saying, "Just one more shot." It's your wedding, and you control the timing. When the bride says, "We have to leave now," everyone heads to the cars.

You're on your way.

CHAPTER 10

At the Wedding

Getting time to visit with guests *during* the wedding? *That's impossible!* At least that's what all of those *other* brides and grooms out there believe. Their friends have told them "You won't even get time to eat, let alone mingle!" And they believe it. So they don't even look at their wedding as anything other than a succession of Big Moments like the first dance, the toasts, cutting the cake, and so on. They expect the five hours to fly by in a flash, and they eliminate all of the wonderful opportunities they actually *do* have to spend time with their friends and family.

You now have a plan. It's going to be different for you. It's going to be *more fun* for you and for your guests.

The key is to make a customized plan for greeting guests during all phases of your wedding celebration. For organization's sake, I've broken this down into the three traditional categories of your reception—the cocktail party, visiting with guests during the reception hours, and sharing dances with your guests—and I encourage you to use the tips in each section *no matter how you've scheduled your own nontraditional celebration.* Yours might not follow the three traditional categories, but you still want to connect with your guests.

> **"** We know we have some eccentric relatives, so we came up with a plan. If either of us is trapped by a chatty guest, the other gets a nearby guest to clink their fork against their water glass a bunch of times to signal that we have to hurry to each other for a kiss. If no one is around to do the clinking, we clink a water glass ourselves, and there's the rescue! Plus, we get to kiss. **"** — *Gavin,* **groom**

You want as many priceless opportunities to really *talk* with people as possible, not just share a quick hug and then awkwardly excuse yourself because you're on your way to speak with someone else you made eye contact with (and yes, that does come across as "someone I want to talk with more than I want to talk with you"). That hurried, distracted greeting as you look back over your shoulder while on your way to someone else, or to the bar, is a big no-no at your wedding. You can't say, "I'll be right back" a hundred times and not let someone down. And you can't hold up your finger in the international sign for "just a second" when a guest has flown a thousand miles to be with you.

Etiquette Basics

Here's your first rule. If you're walking anywhere and a guest stops you, you stop and talk with him or her. No matter where you were headed. If you were on your way to another waiting guest you made eye contact with across the room, just smile their way and nod before turning your attention back to the guest who "got you" first. The guest you were headed toward will get the picture that they, like everyone else, have to allow you to make your way over to them with grace. You'll get there.

Now's a good time to focus on your second key: extracting yourself from a chatty guest. They don't mean to keep you from your other guests. They're just so happy for you and so impressed with the wedding, so in awe of how beautiful you look. And they want to talk with you about it. You'll stay for a short while, *keeping eye contact and not looking around the room* [I know, that part's tough!], and then you'll say, "(Name), I'm so glad you're here, and I'm glad we had a chance to say hello. If you'll excuse me, I need to make my way over to my husband now." Or "I'm making a beeline to the buffet table." And always add, "Be sure to try the (menu item or drink)! I think you're going to love it." Hug, kiss, and then you're outta there.

> **WHAT *NOT* TO SAY** "I'll come back and sit with you," is another no-no, since some guests count on you to keep your word. And with so much going on, you might not be able to keep track of that promise, and some guests will sit down and wait all night, not wanting to miss you. A better phrase is, "(Groom) and I will be coming around to your table shortly, so we'll catch up then!"

If a guest really has your ear, or is actually holding on to your hand, arm, or shoulder as some relatives are apt to do after a few drinks, here's another secret for extracting yourself. Let all of your bridal party members know to keep an eye on you for a rescue. "If you see me pulling my necklace from side to side, that means I need you to step in and say that someone needs to speak with me now, and guide me away from that chatty guest." Your groom can also be alerted to your signal, and invited to create a signal of his own. It could be, "If I'm rubbing my ear, I need outta there." With your inner circle informed, someone can rescue you.

Enough of this focus on getting *away* from guests. Now, with your escape plans all settled, let's focus on how to get you up close and personal with the guests you *want* to talk to.

Mingling at the Cocktail Party

The pre-reception cocktail party can take on many varied forms, depending on your budget and reception site. No matter how it takes shape, you want to make time to greet your guests and actually eat! Here's how.

YOUR ROLE IN THE PARTY

First, let's address the issue of having a receiving line versus attending the party itself. Some couples choose to skip the post-ceremony receiving line so that they have time for lots of picture taking before they go to the cocktail hour. When they do that, they might arrange to hold a receiving line at the entrance to the cocktail party instead. This way, they get to see their guests sooner, their guests get to greet them in an orderly fashion, everyone gets an initial hug as they file into the cocktail party, and you welcome them to your event personally. That's one option that's becoming popular for couples who want their guests to get face time with them right away. So decide whether or not you want the greet-them-at-the-door arrangement, or if you want to be free to take more photos, and then just walk into your cocktail party to mingle freely.

On the other hand, many wedding couples are skipping the main cocktail party or having hors d'oeuvres served to their bridal party and themselves *in a separate room* at the cocktail party location. Some wedding couples loved the drama of being introduced into the reception room to great fanfare. But as you probably know, that first-time-ever introduction still takes place, even if the couple and the bridal party just walk in to the cocktail party and enjoy the fare with their guests. You don't miss a special moment, and you may like the idea of skipping the organized (and endless) receiving line at the entrance to your party.

> " Oh man, if we could do *that* over again, we would skip the receiving line at the entrance to the cocktail party. There we were, greeting guests, and we could smell the amazing food on the buffet tables and being served to all our guests inside. The waiters couldn't even bring us appetizers on platters, because we couldn't eat while greeting our guests, and we could only half-hug people since we were holding our drinks in one hand. It was a *bad* idea. We thought we could greet all of the guests right off the bat, but that was a colossal mistake trying to do it at the entrance to the cocktail party. Bad, bad, bad. " — *Eliza*, newlywed

EATING (YES, YOU CAN EAT!)

Without a receiving line, you're free to walk into the room as soon as your photo session is over, greet guests you see on your path, and get right over to the food before everyone else even knows you're in the room. That's the best way to make sure you get to pick the items for your own plates . . . and load up. Guests will take one look at you, see that you're famished and ready to eat, and hold off on approaching you (at least most of them will). Sit right down at the first available open table, and sample as much of the food as you can. In true partnership fashion, your groom might fill his plate with items from the hot bar, while you fill your plate with items from the cold buffet bar, and you'll share. Yes, you'll get interrupted, and you'll walk away from your plates for a few seconds at a time, but you've made it your mission to get some of your own cocktail party fare to eat.

A great twist on this practice is filling up your plates with cocktail party food, and then retreating together to a side room or the private bridal party suite upstairs (where couples in past years would spend their entire cocktail hour) so that you can chow down and enjoy a few private moments together. Grab a couple of glasses of champagne and have a private "picnic" for two. Forget about parents and others who insist that you not run off alone. This is your time to eat, it's your time to relax, and it's your time to enjoy. You'll only be gone for a few minutes, so parents will just have to wait to introduce you to all the people on their guest lists. Your cocktail party, your way. That's the name of the game.

If you don't have a private room to escape to, arrange with the serving staff to have waiters bring you at least four mini plates of hors d'oeuvres or items from the outside food stations that you haven't been able to get to yet. You have to specifically ask for this when you book your event, and remind the manager the day before the wedding. Consider it a crucial part of your wedding plans. With a dedicated server bringing you snacks, you get to enjoy the food you chose, you get food in your stomach so that drinks don't knock you over, and you don't have any regrets after the wedding that you didn't get to eat a thing. You've got the plan to put into action.

This is not to say that you can't stand in line at the stations of food at the cocktail hour. In fact, that's one of the best ways to get mingling time with your guests. You can chat with the family who flew in from North Carolina as you all await your spring rolls. When you head over to the pasta bar, family and friends will probably let you jump in line ahead of them just for the chance to talk with you while the primavera is being prepped. Consider your food stations to be *mingling* stations.

When you're in line with your guests, *you're* not the center of attention, per se. By talking with guests about the food you're helping yourselves to, you are on an even level with everyone there. You're all just enjoying the party. Guests love that.

> **"**I had the best experience at the cocktail party! I went up to my cousin, who was *taking pictures* of the cocktail party food display and sending them to his friends back home. My husband and I put a lot of money into the food for the wedding, so it was thrilling to see my cousin so excited about the food that he was texting photos of it all! I would have missed that story if I wasn't mingling at the stations. **"**
> — *Carrie Ann*, **newlywed**

Sorry, but you don't get the same effect if you hang out at the bar. It seems like that would be a good place to park yourself and chat with a steady stream of guests who are lining up to get their Chardonnay or Scotch and sodas, but it's actually a misstep. Guests might think you're more interested in drinking than in mingling. So step away from the bar after you get your drinks, or—excellent move here—drinks you've picked up for others, such as grandparents and other honored guests, and continue your mingling where the food is.

HOW *NOT* TO MINGLE AT A COCKTAIL PARTY

What's the number one mistake people make in trying to get more time with guests during the cocktail party? Going from table to table. That may sound like a good way to visit all of your guests, but you're working with moving targets at this party. Everyone is up and about, moving from station to station, mingling with other guests. So trying to get to everyone at the cocktail party isn't effective; besides, *you'll be visiting table to table at the reception.*

And yes, that's a rule, at all weddings. Couples who don't visit tables are seen as rude and ungrateful. Guests shouldn't have to spend time trying to approach you, vying for your time. For now, however, just socialize with whomever crosses your path. Of course, you can sit down with groups of guests out on the terrace or in the cocktail party room. And you can tablehop in a natural flow, without trying to hit every one, which is far more fun for *you* at this point.

If parents come over and push you to go table to table at the cocktail party, use those no-saying skills you learned earlier and let them know you're going table to table later. Parents have a particular talent for being in a rush to get their friends in front of you, so they might be a little bit hyper about pushing you into an orderly mingling pattern during the cocktail hour. That just means the parents could use a cocktail! Just assure them that you have every intention of spending time with every guest and go about your business. "We'll visit your friends' table later on, and you can introduce us all then. Thanks!" and you're off to the Mediterranean bar where your colleagues are gathered. You're not being rude. You're just refusing to be led around the room like a prized pooch as your parents present you to *their* group.

PHOTOS DURING THE COCKTAIL HOUR

Another issue that may come up: parents will want to pull you aside for group photos. Again, put the stall on that plan and let them know that you're going to make time for group photos during the reception, right after the dinner hour, for example.

Just say, "We all have a bunch of group photos we want to take, so we've arranged with the photographer to join us outside in the garden so that we can get those shots taken in an orderly fashion. We don't want to forget any important shots, so it's better to do them all at once." At most receptions, there's a nice chunk of time right after the meal is served and before it's cake time that is *perfect* for family photos. Let your site manager know this is your plan, so that he or she can approach you to let you know there are twenty minutes until cake and dessert will be served. You then gather the family, and it's photo session time.

You're in great control of what happens when. By letting your service staff know your schedule, *they* keep track of it. You can just enjoy your party, and your friends, until your chosen photo time arrives.

DON'T BE A WRECK Don't leave group photos until the end of the reception, because everyone will be disheveled by then— guys' jackets will be off, your bouquet might have already been thrown or presented, and you may be out of those high-heeled shoes for good. The end of the meal is a fine time to snap group photos. Everyone still looks presentable and has energy for more posing.

At the end of the cocktail party, gather your bridal party and parents in the designated area for your grand, dramatic entrance into the reception room if you'd like—or else, just walk in with everyone else without the fanfare, as mentioned earlier. Everyone is already having a fabulous time, many have connected with you and spoken with you, and now it's time to step into the next stage of your unforgettable wedding.

Visiting Guest Tables at the Reception

After the first, official "opening acts" of your reception—which might be your first dance, parents' dances, the best man's and maid of honor's toasts, a cultural offering such as the bread and wine presented by parents, even a special dance number performed by a professional dance troupe or your *own* opening toast presented to your guests—there's a brief period of time perfect for visiting table to table. The servers are getting ready to bring out the first course; the deejay or band plays softer, slower music; and the reception is just gearing up. This is a great time for the two of you to connect with your guests.

Keep in mind that your entertainers might only play the softer, slow-dance songs during the dinner hour, so make sure you don't miss your chance to sway together to your favorite romantic ballads. Visit two or three tables to start—going in numerical order on each side of the dance floor (such as progressing from table 1 to 3 to 5 if your site alternates table numbers on either side of the dance floor, which is often the case so that one family isn't chosen to sit at higher-number tables, such as "tables 10 through 20.") If a song starts that you'd love to dance to, you'll just end your visit time with "This is one of our favorite songs. We'll be back in a little bit." And then you just glide on out to dance. When the song ends, get right back to that table and continue your greetings. Guests love it when they feel like you value them, especially since this is such a big day for you, and you show this by returning to that table for more hugs and hellos.

TALKING WHILE PEOPLE ARE EATING

Over the course of the reception, as food service and the song list allow, go table to table to greet everyone. Now a big question arises: should you stop by a table while everyone is eating? That's up to you. Guests are usually happy to see you approach no matter which stage of their meal they're enjoying, so don't limit your mingling time to only pre- and post-meal service. You'll lose a good hour and a half that way, and you'll feel rushed as you make your way through the tables. As a guideline, try to get to everyone's tables while the meal is being served, since most of your guests will be unlikely to stay at their tables once the dance music begins. Again, a lost opportunity, and a big disappointment to both you and your guests.

WHAT SHOULD YOU SAY?

You or your groom might be a bit nervous about approaching tables of relatives and friends, particularly if there are tables at which you don't know anyone. And it's quite common for a bride or groom not to know the names of some distant relatives and parents' friends, friends' dates, and guests' kids. So agree between yourselves that you won't depend on each other to make introductions outright. You'll introduce *yourselves*, even if it seems silly, since everyone knows who you are. That gets the guest to say who they are. Problem solved. If excited greetings preclude your getting to introduce your spouse to guests who have not yet met him, let that awkward moment pass with a smile and a shrug before making that introduction. Everyone knows your head is probably spinning with all of this activity, so they will be far more likely to excuse you from social proprieties. As the bride and groom, you have an out in that regard.

Arm yourselves with some conversation starters. "These are my cousins from Alabama," you might say, "They're big Crimson Tide fans." If your groom is a fan as well, there's the common link for a friendly exchange.

You will hear "Everything is wonderful!" and "You look so beautiful!" and "The food is amazing!" from just about all of your guests, so prepare to be showered with compliments. A simple "Thank you" is all that's needed, along with "The staff here did an amazing job!" or "Our wedding coordinator is fantastic." It's never a great idea to launch into stories about how much trouble you had with the planning, what went wrong at the last moment, what you *wish* you could have planned, or other gory details. That's not a way to connect well with your guests, and it makes you sound ungrateful and impossible to please, even if that's not your intention. Why would you be so negative right now? Guests want to share your joy, not feel like you're trying to pull compliments (or sympathy) out of them! So be aware of this common couple-chat mistake, so that your table-to-table visits are uplifting and joyful. That means asking guests about *themselves.*

"How was your trip out here?"

"How do you like the hotel? Did you get a chance to visit the spa?"

And of course, you'll let every guest know how happy you are to see them, how thrilled you are that they made it.

And off you go to the next table.

> **❝**We looked at our guest list and decided in advance to plan an extended visit time with friends from out-of-state whom we don't get to see all the time. We picked the names, kept it to just five or six couples so that we didn't feel overwhelmed with a to-do list, and it worked out perfectly. Better to have a plan than to wing it.**❞** — *Charlie,* newlywed

For your closest friends and long-distance relatives who top your Socializing Priority List, you'll assure them that you're going to make the rounds right now, but you want to make sure to get time to talk. One secret to assuring the mingling time you want is to tell guests, "We'll come sit with you during dessert. Don't let us get distracted. Just call us over." That's the magic phrase. Guests now know you want to have sit-down time with them, so they're more likely to call you over when they see you passing by.

Don't be afraid to give your guests permission to flag you down. They're your allies in granting your wish to spend time with them.

DON'T FORGET ABOUT *YOUR* MEAL

Tell your manager that you'd like the servers to come find you when they place your meal at your table. It's a common mistake among brides and grooms who *don't* make this request that their meals are placed at the table without them knowing, and by the time they look over, their filet mignon is cold. Don't skip this step and risk missing your own gratifying, indulgent entrée. This also provides you with an automatic "out" from whatever conversation you're having if you need one.

After the meal is served, there's usually another lull in the food service action before the cake and desserts, so this is your time to mingle some more. Most couples decide they don't need to be joined at the hip throughout the entire reception, and they each head off in separate directions to visit with their friends and family members. You're covering double the ground this way and getting to spend your reception time the way you want to. Yes, it's wonderful to meet and chat with your groom's college friends, but once they get into reminiscing, you are perfectly within your rights to excuse yourself and visit with friends of your own. Again, everyone grants you the freedom to move about as you wish. They know you only have so much time, so no one will mind if you step away from the table.

DON'T FORGET TO MAKE FULL USE OF THE GROUNDS

If guests are seated outside on the terrace, especially on a gorgeous day, go out there and join them. Your photographer may just pop up to snap a few priceless photos of you as a group. If friends are seated out in the gardens, visit with them. Or sit on the dramatic staircase in the lobby with some guests. You all get to enjoy the scenery and you will likely get some great photo opportunities too. It may be your professional photographer, and it may be a friend with a camera—it doesn't matter.

> " Some of the best moments of our reception were when we stepped outside and joined our friends for a drink out on the terrace. Our site overlooked a lake, so we all walked out onto the pier, got away from the loud music inside, and had fabulous visiting time. And someone took a photo of us walking out onto the pier, which became one of our favorite photos of all. We had a copy made for the friends who were with us, and they love it too. " — *Tania*, **newlywed**

Don't forget that the reception might not be your only time to visit with friends. If you've planned an after-party, you know you're going to get hours of mingling time with them later, so you can put more focus and effort into visiting with family members, your bosses and colleagues, and the in-laws as the reception rolls on.

If you allow yourselves to be *guided* by your wishes to spend more time with guests, and you don't get too militant about it, you'll find yourselves in a comfortable flow of sticking with your mingling plan *and* still sharing quality time together. Agree at the start, "If one of us really wants to dance, the other steps away from guests to do so." You're aiming for balance, not sacrificing bride-and-groom time, as you enjoy moments with your most cherished friends and family. Tip the scales too far either way, and you turn into the very thing you're trying to eliminate.

Dancing with VIP Guests

It might not be enough for you just to sit down and talk with your most special guests. You might have a big wish to dance with them. If you're going to dance with your parents, why not dance with grandparents, favorite aunts and uncles, each other's parents? That's a big one. Too many couples stick with the Expected Dance List of bride with her father and groom with his mother, and they miss out on the chance to dance with the in-laws and get great photos of those moments. This is your reception, your way. So your spotlight dances should be your way as well.

> " It's always been a big thing for my family to dance to a cha-cha at every wedding we've been to. My parents really know how to cut up the dance floor with a great cha-cha, and the rest of us have learned from them. So I made a special request at my wedding that my family join us on the dance floor for that spotlight dance, the first cha-cha my new husband would ever do with us! Talk about an initiation into the family! " —*Leanne*, newlywed

There's no need to dedicate special songs for these dances, since you don't want the emcee to clear the floor for you to dance with Uncle Harry. Just approach your special guest's table as an appropriate song is playing and hold out your hand as you invite that guest to join you on the dance floor. Other guests almost trample each other to capture that great moment on their cameras, and your special guest will be elated that you want to dance during your special day when your time is precious.

Who is on your special dance list? Slow dances are ideal for the older generation, although it can be great fun to get Grandpa out there, shaking it to the songs you hear at nightclubs. Groups of friends might be called out to dance with you, and you can certainly invite your families to join you as you dance to a song that's a special part of your family history.

> " My mom never got the memo that the Dollar Dance, in which guests pay a dollar to dance with the bride, is offensive and outdated. She pressured us so much to include it. We said no over and over again, and we tipped off our deejay that he was to say no when she approached *him* to try to get him to announce the Dollar Dance at the reception. She tried. The deejay said no. And when she appealed to us because it would 'make her day,' we saw it as the power play that it was. *That* was going to make her day? Give me a break. We would hate ourselves right now if we gave in on that one. " —*Anya*, **newlywed**

Child guests often can't get enough of the bride. You look like a princess to the little girls, and when you welcome the kids on the dance floor with you, that makes them feel special. Brides often express how much they loved dancing with the little ones, as they twirled in their party dresses and showed off their dance moves. If you're among the couples who plan weddings where kids are not only allowed but encouraged to attend, this might be your favorite VIP dance group. Even if it's just the flower girls at your wedding, they will love sharing the spotlight with you. The ring bearers and other boys may enjoy the spotlight as well, and they can show off their best dance moves with you *and* the groom. But, of course, be ready for a shy shake of the head from *any* child guest you invite for a dance.

> " We've been to dozens of weddings where the deejay or band actually *defied* the bride and groom's wishes about no cheesy dances, and the first relative who requested one got it played. You could see the bride and groom deflate. Someone overruled them on their wedding day. And you could see the videographer turn off the camera. Not a moment to immortalize. So we told our deejay that if he plays any cheesy songs on our Do Not Play List, we won't tip him. At all. There was no Chicken Dance, Macarena, Electric Slide, conga line, or any other cheesy song played at our wedding. Success! " — *Marcia and Ben*, **newlyweds**

Some brides and grooms have even been known to step up on the stage and dance with the band. Who says you can't join them? If they're rocking the house, get right up there and dance with them! Some brides will join the backup singers and sing along. Some brides and grooms will take lead vocals over from the band singer—just for a song, not for a concert. Some sit in with the band, stepping behind the drum set for a while if welcomed by the drummer. Entertainers *love* it when they're making you so happy that you want to be one of them. So free yourselves to join in. And that includes any line dances that you approve.

Hear that again. Any line dances *that you approve.*

Again, there's a bit of a danger zone when a parent or guest *loves* the Chicken Dance and wants it at your wedding, even though it's on your Don't Play List. You do have one of those, right? If not, write one up and make sure your band or deejay receives it weeks before the wedding. There will be no songs that remind you of exes, or your divorced parents' wedding song, or that blasted Chicken Dance. Others may say you're overreacting when you don't want a line dance played at your wedding, but it's not the others' day. If they want a Chicken Dance, they can do it at their own daughter's wedding. You won't be bullied, and you won't be the first wedding couple to experience the Chicken Dance Crisis or the Great Macarena Battle.

It's your wedding, your way. So if line dances are not your style, they remain on the Don't Play List.

Now if you're a Macarena connoisseur, by all means enjoy sharing your wished-for wedding moment with your friends and family. The rules are yours to make, and you know the steps to make them.

CHAPTER 11

After the Wedding

In years past, the bride and groom cut their wedding cake, danced a few more dances, and then made a grand exit to their awaiting getaway car, whisking them off to their bridal suite for privacy. But most of today's brides and grooms put that privacy on hold, choosing instead *not* to leave the party early. "We don't want to miss a minute with our guests!" is their rationale for doing away with the age-old tradition of early departure from the party. There are a *lot* more songs to dance to, a lot more hugs to exchange, more hours of sitting down with special guests they may not have seen in years. And that dessert bar is still open.

Now, it's far more common for the bride and groom to close down their own reception, being there to say goodbye to every guest headed out the door. They don't miss a moment of their big day. Compare that to couples from decades ago who missed *hours*. It can be hard to believe anyone ever agreed to the early departure plan, but those were the days when couples were eager to rush off to their marriage bed. In those chaste days, couples didn't live together before marriage and sleeping together—actually *sleeping* together—was a rite of passage. Let's just say we're a bit removed from those times. But still, until rather recently, couples still held to the tradition of leaving the reception early. It was, after all, what they were *supposed to do.*

If you're like most brides and grooms of today, you're not planning on leaving early. You're not going to miss a song, even if it *is* "The Chicken Dance Song." You're staying until the end of the party, and then some.

The After-Party

Yes, this is what *and then some* means: an after-party, a planned get-together for *after* the reception. You might be thinking, "Wait, we just put on an ultra-expensive wedding celebration that lasted all day and all night, and now we're going to host *another* party?" Before you panic about any new trauma on your credit cards, be assured that the after-party is more about *time* spent with people, not *money* spent *on* people. The after-party has evolved to give you more quality time with your faraway friends and relatives in a more relaxed atmosphere that has *no* distractions and none of the formality of the wedding celebration itself. You can change out of your wedding gown, and your groom out of his tux, into more casual clothes, and host or meet up with your similarly dressed-down bridal party members and friends at the hotel lounge. Or have everyone come back to your place for drinks and snacks.

The after-party has become so popular that many couples consider it an absolute must. And they enjoy planning it as much as they enjoyed putting together the cocktail party, the rehearsal dinner, or any other guest-centric event on the wedding weekend. I say "guest-centric," because that's the focus of this get-together:

more time to spend with your guests. Make that more *comfortable* time to spend with your guests. Everyone can step out of those high heels and perhaps slip into a bathing suit for an evening dip in your backyard pool. Some couples invite their after-party VIP guests back to their honeymoon suite for a few hours of socializing and snacks. If someone brings along the leftover cheese platter and some bottles of wine from the reception, it's a double-duty menu for this new party!

DETERMINING FORMALITY

Let's start off by looking at the different styles of after-parties for you to consider:

- **Casual:** Everyone changes out of their formalwear into shorts and tee shirts or bathing suits for a laid-back get-together at your place, a hotel room, or a friend's home. You'll have drinks and snacks, and everyone gets a few hours of relaxed mingling time, maybe even turning on ESPN to catch highlights of the day's games.
- **Dress-Up:** Hey, everyone spent good money on those new dresses, suits, and shoes, so let's get them out into the public eye where they can be appreciated—and maybe your single guests can get some quality flirtations in with the bartender at the hotel lounge or your favorite nightclub. Since all of your friends are dressed their best, you'd rather hit the town in heels than hit the couches in sweatpants. Bridal parties especially get a *lot* of attention out in the bars and clubs, so don't forget to give your nearest and dearest their own time to shine. You were the star of the day, now they can get their dose of attention on the dance floor.

Now that you have your formality level set, it's time to share the wealth here. *Parents* and other friends and relatives can host their own after-parties! A wedding often brings long-distance relatives into town for the first time in years, and your parents will surely want more than a few, distracted, interrupted hours with their closest cousins, siblings, and friends. Grandparents too love the option of having all of their loved ones at a *quieter*, at-home party.

> " When our daughter first suggested that we host an after-party at our house, we originally thought it would be overkill, that we would already have had plenty of time with our relatives, but it was shocking how quickly the cocktail party went by, and then with all the dancing and greeting guests, we got almost *no* time to sit and talk with family. So it was a blessing that we had invited the relatives back to our place for a post-party of coffee and desserts from the wedding. " — *Eleanor*, **mother of the bride**

WHO'S INVITED?

Since the after-party is all about the people you want to share time with, who is going to be on your VIP list? Obviously, with a 300-person wedding guest list, you can't host *everyone* back at your place, out at a club or in your hotel suite, so a careful guest list creation begins here.

This task might make you a little bit nervous, and here you are again, facing the issue of "what will people expect?" or "who will we be expected to include?" Just like your wedding guest list, this VIP guest list may pose a few challenges when you take your space and budget into consideration. With all of the cousins in town, how do you invite the three with whom you're closest without offending all the rest? The answer: you just do it. This is *your* party, and there's no reason why you would invite little-known cousins whose names you don't even know, plus their spouses, and their kids, back to your suite for a nightcap. The extended cousins know you're close to those other cousins, so the lack of an invitation is something they'll just have to get over . . . if they know about the after-party at all.

Now here's a little secret: Give all out-of-town guests a list of some great, nearby lounges that they can arrange to go to together. Suggest it. Let them know that the hotel bar has great martinis and a fantastic wine list. They can form their own after-party. Just be sure that *your* party will take place someplace other than the hotel lounge, or you'll have a lot of extra guests whose drinks will wind up on your tab. With your party taking place at home, and your hotel guests at the bar downstairs, everyone's happy.

Who else gets on the VIP list? Your bridal party, of course, plus their dates.

THE BUS LINE FORMS HERE Yikes! Don't offend your many wedding guests by making it too obvious that a select group has been invited to a post-party . . . and there they all are, waiting in line for the shuttle bus to take them to the marina for a midnight cruise. Be a little more careful about group departures, because friends *do* notice when blocks of people are in line for a VIP "phase two" of the evening. You don't want to end your big day by *inviting* scorn and hurt feelings.

You and your spouse can also invite siblings to join your group, unless they choose to go to a family member's house to spend time with the guests. It might be that your brother wants to spend more time with your grandparents or have his kids spend more time with your grandparents. Everyone gets to spell out their own priorities.

With your friends, invite your closest to the after-party, and make it a hush-hush thing. Tell your closest friends that you aren't able to invite *all* of your other friends and acquaintances to your place for a post-party, so you'd appreciate their discretion.

A smaller guest list is always best, and the natural inclusions will form as you write out your list. Out-of-town friends, *check.* The bridal party, *check.* It can be a very good idea to create a tiered list for this party, just as you may have done for your wedding guest list. Bridal party is tier 1, college friends are tier 2, your best work friends are tier 3, close cousins are tier 4, and then you get into colleagues with whom you're not very close, distant relatives, acquaintances, and so on. Set a solid cutoff number, such as the thirty people you'd most comfortably host in your hotel suite or at your house, and draw the line there.

IT'S ALL IN THE TIMING

One very important factor in planning your after-party is the timing. Just a minute ago, you read about the danger of having your after-party guests lined up for a shuttle, in full view of other, uninvited guests. That immediately-after-the-ceremony timing created an awkward scenario and potential family and friend troubles for you. But if your after-party was not scheduled for *immediately* after your reception, and had that shuttle not been planned to depart from your reception parking lot, the whole matter could have been avoided. That's just one illustration of timing: delaying the start or departure to the party until a short while later helps you keep the secrecy factor, and aids in keeping the peace.

Here are some other timing considerations:

- Allowing your after-party guests to join the others in heading back to the hotel via the shuttle allows them the chance to change into different outfits, relax a little bit, maybe sober up a little bit as well.

- Planning the after-party to begin two hours after the reception allows *you* the chance to go back to your hotel room or home, change into going-out or relaxing clothes, enjoy a bit of private time together, unpack your wedding gifts safely into your home, and perhaps walk and feed your pets that have been housebound all day. You just get a little breathing time. A few hours later, you can join your friends at the nightclub or look forward to your after-party guests' arrival at your place—which you've now had a chance to clean up a little bit after the whirlwind of getting ready this morning, taking photos, and preparing to head to the ceremony. Maybe that sink full of coffee cups and breakfast plates can be cleared, the dishwasher run, and your party preparations set out.

- If your guests will begin the after-party in another friend's hotel room or at another guest's home, you can take the same hour or two to change clothes, relax, unload those gifts, and then join your already-partying friends when you're ready.

- If several guests, including your parents, will host after-parties of their own, perhaps the two of you can make the rounds and visit several of them throughout the course of the evening.

- If you have an afternoon wedding that ends at 5 P.M., that means your after-party will take on more of a cocktail party style, with food served. If your wedding ends at 11 P.M., then the after-party will obviously be more late-night friendly with desserts or even breakfast food served, and you do have the option of a cocktail party with appetizers as well.

- A late-night after-party might stir up a dilemma: your guests may have RSVP'd that they would attend your late-night bash, and you may have shopped for enough food to feed thirty people, but after your amazing reception, guests find that they are too tired to attend, or too drunk to drive to your house. This is something to consider when you plan a late-night party or expect guests to come to your place in the late-night hours.

LOCATION, LOCATION

The first step is figuring out where you'll have the party.

At the Hotel

I've already mentioned that your after-party can take place in your hotel suite ("Look at that view!"), at the hotel lounge, at your home, or at a friend's home or hotel room. I highly suggest, though, that you think about the ramifications of hosting an after-party in your honeymoon suite or at your home. You might think you'll have plenty of energy, but even a blissful, perfect wedding day can be exhausting. All the activity and stress of the months leading to the big day can crash down on the wedding couple right at the end of the reception, and many couples say they regretted hosting the after-party at their home or hotel room because they were drained.

LATE-NIGHT LOCATION? It's often best to keep the after-party close to your guests' hotel, even *in* the hotel such as at the lounge or at a friend's hotel room, so that you don't lose VIP guests to the hassles—and dangers—of driving after your wedding.

Plus, they couldn't escape from this late-night party, since they didn't want to throw out their partying guests. So they pounded some espresso and stayed up all night. Add in the mess of a party you'd have to clean up afterward, your potential need to wake up early for a honeymoon flight (or to pack for the trip!), and neighbors' displeasure at your loud guests, and this "great idea" could be anything but. So think about after-party challenges and details. Perhaps a different location (or hosts!) might work better for you.

TURN THE KEG AROUND, MA'AM And here's another thing to keep in mind: some hotels don't allow you to bring in outside food and drink. They'll stop you in the parking lot to prevent partiers from walking into the building with kegs and cases. The hotel may insist you get all drinks and food through them.

At Your Parents' or Relative's House

Parents have been known to thrill at the chance to show off their homes to their own party guest lists. They might have an amazing backyard pool or hot tub that's the perfect setting for a post-wedding party. Many family groups have just spontaneously gathered at the parents' place, with the happy hosts willingly busting out their wine collections and dialing out for pizza deliveries. Some of the best after-parties are spontaneous. And friends and relatives have been known to do the same, extending a verbal "Hey, come back to our place" at the close of your successful and unforgettable wedding reception.

It's now become a big trend for nearby friends and relatives to host after-parties as well, with so many members of your group in town for the first time in years. And at-home entertaining has never been more popular. In fact, many married couples invest a huge amount of money in making their homes and yards party-ready. "All the family's going to be in town? Great! Let's have everyone over for drinks after the wedding!" The at-home after-party is a hot trend, with everyone wanting to share their homes with friends and family, and—this is the fun part—as a way to take any planning pressure or expense off of *you*. With them hosting the party, you don't have to plan another event. Hopefully, they'll check with you first to make sure they're not committing any etiquette faux pas, but as long as their plans don't clash with yours, you may have the ideal after-party location: someone else's place!

> **"** After we shelled out for our gowns, shoes, a shower, and all kinds of other bridesmaid expenses, the four of us bridesmaids talked about what we could give the bride and groom as a great wedding present. We knew friends were giving $300 cash gifts, and we couldn't afford that individually. So we decided to give the happy couple the gift of a no-worries, no-work after-party in our hotel suite with a few sandwich platters, a case of wine and some mixed drinks, and a tray of brownies for dessert. The entire event came up to just over $300 *total* for the five of us to host, so it worked out really well, and the bride and groom *loved* it that we planned this post-party for them. **"** —*Sarah*, **bridesmaid**

At Your House

Before you plan your after-party for your house, take a minute to assess if it's really realistic for you to host a party at your place on the night of your wedding:

- Will you be dressing and prepping for the wedding at your place on the morning of the wedding, with breakfast plates everywhere, hairspray bottles left out on the counter? Or will you get ready at another location, meaning that your place could potentially be clean and ready for guests?

- Will you have time to shop for party supplies, such as paper plates and napkins, before the wedding date, or do you have plenty of your own dinnerware and wine glasses to suit your guest list?

- Would you have to rent wine glasses and plates, chairs and other items for a big-group party? When would those need to be dropped off and delivered back to the rental agency? (For some couples, this is a deal breaker)

- Do you have light-colored carpet and furniture that you'd hate to get marred by red wine stains? If you're leaving for your honeymoon at 6 A.M. the next morning, professional carpet cleaners would never be able to get that stain out of your carpet. Your house might not be suitable for tipsy guests to be eating and drinking there right before your honeymoon.

- Is there enough seating room for everyone?

- Does your neighborhood or apartment building have strict rules about noise violations? Your cranky neighbors could make a complaint, and you could come home from your honeymoon to find you're being evicted because of a loud party.

- Will you have enough refrigerator space for platters of food for *this* party, in addition to the space you'll need for the wedding morning food, drinks, etc? This one too is often a deal breaker when couples figure out it would be way too much of a hassle to store giant platters, or go through the trouble of heating up food in their kitchens for the party.

This should help to get you thinking about whether or not your home is the best place for this party.

At Another Location

Some other options for after-parties? Couples have headed out en masse to local jazz clubs to take in a musical performance. The couple pays for everyone's cover change and then everyone splits the bar and food bill. On a lower budget, how about heading to the nearest sports bar to join a rowdy crowd watching the big game? You in your gown and your groom in his tux shooting pool or throwing darts at a dartboard? Priceless photos.

For late-late parties, groups have been known to go to the local diner for burgers, fries, and shakes, just like they used to do in high school and college.

If you live near or on the beach, your group can sit on blankets and watch the sun come up. Just be sure it's a public beach where you wouldn't be trespassing and that you don't have alcohol with you. Many beach communities have strict laws on that, and you wouldn't want to spend your after-party in the county jail.

WHAT'S ON THE MENU?

That's up to you to decide and arrange. Here are some popular options:

- Many wedding couples arrange to take their reception food home with them. At the after-party, they can bring out platters for their guests' second helpings. And those who are immediately leaving on their honeymoon invest in plastic take-home containers for their guests to load up on leftovers, rather than let them spoil in the fridge.
- The second most popular option is getting party platters at discount stores like Costco. You can choose sandwich and seafood platters, wraps, salads, bread, and big boxes of donuts or cookies for dessert. Self-catering *cold* menu items means big bargains and a lot less work. It would be a nightmare to have to fire up your oven and time the heating process for trays of pasta or meat dishes.

Just like with the pre-wedding lunch, sandwich bars are also hot picks. Just buy lots of different kinds of rolls and cold cuts, plus fresh salads and pickles and an array of chips, and your guests get to make their own sandwiches. Make it healthier and more unique by buying tortillas instead of rolls and guests can make their own wraps.

- Choose a family-style offering, like a lasagna (if you want to take on the heating-up task) or a big pot of chili, and set out a salad and some bread for a sit-down comfort food indulgence.

> " What a disaster! We thought it would be easy to order a bunch of trays of chicken, some shrimp and other finger foods for the after-party, but when we put the trays in the oven, some of the pasta sauce bubbled over and got on the bottom of the oven, where it started to burn and filled our house with smoke. " — *Claire and Bryan,* newlyweds

- And there's always the old, reliable pizza order, which is often the most popular choice for after-parties. It's not just the ease of ordering, or the paper-plates serving style that makes this a winner. Guests might say, "We can't get good pizza where we live, and this area has great pizza!" or "I haven't been back to my hometown in years, and I really miss Joe's Pizza, so this is a great opportunity for me to enjoy it and share it with my new spouse." The pizza may be as big a hit as your reception fare. And if it's not pizza that your region is known for, make it some other order-in area specialty such as gumbo or pulled pork sandwiches. Some hosts whip out their collection of delivery menus and let guests order what they want from the menus, such as sushi from one place, and chicken sandwiches from another. The generous hosts pay the bills when each delivery person arrives, and the crowd feasts.
- Another trend is a desserts-only party, which you'll self-cater by getting trays of pastries, a few pies, fruit salad, chocolate mousse,

chocolate-dipped strawberries, and other baked treats. Some couples load up on boxes of Entenmann's to give their guests a wide range of choices—donuts, a cheese ring, or chocolate chip cookies. Then, they fire up the espresso or cappuccino maker they received as a shower gift, pour the after-dinner liqueurs, and it's an indulgent dessert party.

- Speaking of coffee, your late-night bash might be better served as a breakfast-foods buffet. If frozen waffles are not your style, perhaps everyone can join together in the kitchen to whip up some eggs, bacon, pancakes and the like. Egg melt sandwiches—containing scrambled eggs, a round of Canadian bacon, and melted cheese—are always popular with the been-out-drinking crowd. As is that Mickey Mouse waffle iron you've had for many years. Again, boxes of Entenmann's donuts or Dunkin' Donuts muffins can be bought fresh on the morning of the wedding—or leftover—from your wedding-morning breakfast with the bridesmaids—and you can also get terrific pastry platters from your bakery, grocery store, Costco, or Sam's Club, ready and waiting for your post-reception revelers, at a very low price.

WHAT'S TO DRINK?

At any party, the host pays for drinks. That's the going rule with wedding etiquette. But when you're with your closest friends, and you're all at a sports bar, you might all agree to split the tab. Your friends might insist on it. Outside of this familiar circle, you should always plan to pay for the entire drink bill. If you're at a bar or restaurant, arrange with the server to bring over a set number of wine bottles over the course of your party. Servers are usually more than happy to be on the receiving end of such a big order, so ask to be notified when you've gone through six bottles, or x number of mixed drinks just to keep on top of your tab and not get stunned by a four-figure bar tab.

You might be able to take the wine, liquor, and beer you purchased for the reception and use them for this party, or you might visit a discount liquor store to stock up on a nice variety of wines and cases of beer. If your party is small, you might decide just to use the collection of liquors and wines you already own—clear some space on that wine rack for bottles you'll buy while on your honeymoon.

> " Since our wedding was so formal, we really wanted to surprise our guests with what we considered to be something silly at the after-party. So we went to the party supply store and loaded up on cups, plates, and napkins in what we judged to be the silliest theme in the store, a kids' cartoon character. When guests saw it, we just said, 'After that wedding, we had to lighten it up a bit!' " —*Stacy and Paul,* **newlyweds**

At the end of the night, guests who enjoyed liquor at the reception may find they've reached their limit, and they may want to rehydrate with a selection of nonalcoholic drinks. So here are some options to stock: bottles of water, bottles of flavored iced tea, pink lemonade mix, gourmet sodas such as Fizzy Lizzy, Izze, and Steaz in wonderful flavors such as pomegranate and green apple, plus sodas like root beer, birch beer, ginger ale, and sarsaparilla to give your guests a unique soft drink taste.

Coffees and teas may run the flavor gamut as well, so look into tasty syrups such as French vanilla, hazelnut, and berry. Remember to run both caffeine and decaf pots of coffee to suit your guests, and use either your fine coffee cups or fun, themed coffee cups from the party supply store.

ENTERTAINMENT

At the jazz club, the musicians provide the entertainment. At the nightclub or sports bar, it's going to be the deejay. At your place or in your hotel suite, entertainment is up to you. Very few couples plan an after-party where they hire a musician or deejay, although you may hear that some big-budget couples do bring in professional entertainment for their post-wedding party. To those couples, enjoy! But for the rest of us, it's time to pull out your iPod and dock to run your playlist or load your CD player with your favorite discs. If your television cable server offers channels that play music divided into categories of Soft Jazz, Classic Rock, Party Songs, or Today's Hits, you might want to just click on your favorite channel and let the TV provide your party playlist.

There are those who like to drag out the karaoke machine for their guests' amusement, and this is the ideal evening of togetherness for a rousing rendition of "Every Little Thing She Does Is Magic." If you don't own a karaoke machine, perhaps a friend would be willing to bring his over for the party.

VIEWING PARTY

Your friends and guests will likely show you the photos they took on their digital cameras, and you may have the technology to arrange for a slideshow on your television so that everyone can see. It's a top trend at after-parties to share those candid photos with the group, and friends who took video may be able to display that footage for all of you as well. This footage might have funny greetings, hysterical renditions of the cha-cha slide, and sentimental footage of your group sharing the first toast of the evening.

Be sure to share all of these ideas with your parents for their after-party as well, so that they can entertain their friends and relatives in style, in flavor and perhaps even with their own karaoke machine!

When it's time to call it a night, make sure everyone has a safe ride home, and while party favors are not required, a packaged take-home favor is a cute idea you might even find at that party supply store. Who doesn't need a cartoon-character Pez dispenser for the ride home?

The Morning-After Brunch

Since today's weddings are all about making sure that guests have a great time from start to finish, the tradition of offering a morning-after breakfast or brunch has become a must. Of course, since this is your wedding, your way, you can choose to do what you like. Here is some information on how to go about planning one if you do want to have one.

AT THE HOTEL

On the morning after the wedding celebration, guests are invited to attend a breakfast that is most often held in the hotel in which they are staying. Many hotels feature a regular Saturday morning *and* Sunday morning brunch buffet that can be as simple as a few chafing dishes of scrambled eggs, bacon, sausage, and French toast or as lavish as the menu from your cocktail party — simmering salmon encrusted with fried onions, a sushi or spring roll bar, marinated chicken strips, a prime rib carving station, pasta dishes, salads, and a dessert bar that might be more extensive than what you had at your reception. Many hotels bring out pies, cakes, pastries, an ice cream bar for the kids, all for a stunningly low per-person price. This is often seen as the perfect send-off and an indulgent meal for guests who traveled to attend your fete, gave generous gifts, and booked rooms at the hotel for the entire weekend. And we all know how valuable everyone's weekends are to them. So the morning-after breakfast has become a top-notch way to treat them one more time.

Since this morning-after event has become such a big deal, you'll now find that *parents* often want to claim this party all to themselves as hosts and planners, especially if they feel left out of the wedding plans and preparations. You have, after all, planned your wedding your way. This morning-after event could be on their radar as the one thing that's going to be *their* way. If your parents hosted an engagement party for you, and your groom's parents took on the rehearsal dinner, there may be a competition for who gets *this* party. And you have every right to say, as you have said before, "No, this one's going to be our way as well."

WHO SHOULD HOST IT?

Don't worry about another heaping serving of resentment and parents jockeying for position as you hold yet another wished-for plan out of their reach (at least this is how some parents may see it). The good news is it's now okay for the bride and groom to host a breakfast while the parents host their own. You can have yours at the hotel where your friends are staying, and your parents can have it at their home, in a separate party room at the same hotel, or just in a separate room of the hotel restaurant. You each get to plan your own guest lists, seating charts, and decorations. If the parties are in the same hotel at the same time, you could visit both but spend the majority of the breakfast with your closest out-of-town friends. Your bill amounts to just what your group consumed, and your parents' tables are the only ones charged to them. Everyone's happy.

This works out much better than if Mom and Dad invite fifty relatives to a breakfast at their house, which would require you to *leave* your friends after a quick gulp of coffee and join their party.

Too many wedding couples of the past have had to do just that. They were pressured to follow along with their parents' plans for the morning-after breakfast out of guilt that they ran most of the actual wedding their way.

This split party in the same location prevents you from missing one minute with your friends. It's the best of all worlds, since everyone plans for their own tables and groupings of guests.

> **"** When my parents went ahead and planned a big hotel-based morning-after breakfast and sent out invitations to all the relatives, we worried at first about how we would ever be able to spend morning time with *our* friends . . . who weren't invited. So we took a look at the invitation: Mom and Dad's breakfast started at 9 A.M. We quickly figured out that we could go to that party from 9 A.M. to 10 A.M., and *then* we would join our friends at a breakfast that started *at* 10:30 A.M. elsewhere. We have a favorite diner nearby, so we hosted our ten out-of-town friends and bridal party members there, which they didn't have to wake up early to attend. **"** — *Tricia and Paul,* newlyweds

The timing of the different events will probably work in your favor as well. Parents who wish to host breakfasts at their homes or at the hotel often want the earlier hours of 8 A.M. to 10 A.M., thinking that most of their peers will surely want to eat breakfast and then get an early start for home. That's fine planning, and very considerate to guests who have already spent the majority of the weekend with you. Your friends might not awaken until 11 A.M., so they'll be very happy with a brunch or lunch plan that might not start until late morning or early afternoon.

You can even host both parties at the same place. Your parents' hotel-based breakfast takes place in festivity and delight with that great array of brunch food and free mimosas, and as they start departing, your next round of guests start arriving. Your hotel events specialist can easily help you plan two parties on the same day! They're not going to fight you on their opportunity to make double the money! So you might be able to book the hotel's brunch area atrium for your parents and their friends, and then a separate seating area or party room for your friends. By virtue of having both parties at the same place, you're not hopping in your car to speed off to that diner—or to prep a party at your home with just an hour of time between events.

So do you want to battle the parents for control over one unified breakfast, or suggest that everyone plan and host their own groups at the same place? In many cases, both sets of parents are happier to be able to host their own separate brunches (even if you have one as well). After all, if you have one giant brunch, the parents might be reduced (in their minds) to just guests who happen to bring a veggie quiche.

WHAT TO SAY TO YOUR PARENTS

When it comes to approaching parents with your plan for separate-but-equal and local breakfast parties, here's a script that works: "We've been thinking about the morning-after brunch plans and how it would work best for us all to handle our wishes for that event. So here's what we have in mind, and we think it works beautifully. You, (groom's parents), and we will each create our own guest lists for our own tables or sections of the hotel restaurant, and we each have our own self-hosted breakfast gatherings right there. You can have the atrium or the outdoor terrace, or whichever location you want" (note that parents like to be given this big choice up front). "And we'll grab a corner of the restaurant or their small party room just off the main dining room. This way, we each get full creative control, our own guest lists, and the price tag gets cut in thirds. We'll all handle our own tabs, and everyone gets to spend time together, even if your earlier party overlaps with our breakfast starting later in the morning. It couldn't be better. Do you agree?"

LOCATION IDEAS

I've spent a lot of time focusing on the morning-after brunch as if there was only one option: holding it at the hotel where the guests are staying. Yes, that's a bright idea, since it makes it easy for guests to attend and everyone gets to the food faster. Plus, when you book a room block at the hotel, many hotel catering managers will give you a hefty per-person discount on the cost of the brunch. Here's an opportunity to enjoy great service, great food, and the VIP status of being the bride and groom at this out-in-public breakfast party.

> **WHAT TO WEAR** Some brides wear their "The New Mrs. Smith" T-shirt they bought or were gifted by their bridal parties to the morning-after brunch. Now's the time for your "we're married" personalization, whatever that may be.

As enticing as the hotel breakfast buffet might be for your trio of parties, or for one big breakfast bash if your parents agree to an equal cohosting plan with full harmony and joy for you (and aren't you lucky to have that!), you might find that the hotel buffet prices are still a bit too steep for your big guest list. It might be a better option to host an at-home morning-after breakfast.

You could host it at *your* home. Or it might be held at a parent's party-friendly home. (Perhaps they always host the big family holidays, and they have the great kitchen and huge dining table, an outdoor kitchen by the pool, or other attractive feature.)

> ❝ We spent a year designing our back terrace to be the site of our wedding-morning breakfast with a caterer on hand and servers walking around with breakfast foods, champagne, shrimp cocktail, and the like. We picked our *wedding date* to suit the fall morning we envisioned for this event. After all, we had to change our plans for a back-yard wedding because our guest list got too big . . . so this plan allowed us to bring our backyard catered party dream to life, and everyone had a blast. ❞ — *Tasha and Alan,* newlyweds

Planning Your Breakfast, Your Way

The morning-after breakfast offers you the chance to use any ideas, themes, and even menu items that you couldn't work into your wedding plans. It may have been a size issue like Tania and Alan experienced, a budget issue, or a disagreement on style and formality between yourselves. Your idea for a champagne bar may have been too pricey for the rehearsal dinner your in-laws are hosting, but it's perfect for this breakfast of yours. Just like your wedding, this event should reflect your wishes and style. Now let's get into planning it . . .

HOW TO PLAN A HOTEL BREAKFAST/BRUNCH

- When you call to investigate hotel room block prices, ask if they offer a discount on their morning-after brunch pricing for guests.
- Ask if that discount applies only to guests of the hotel, or to all of your guests, including those who live nearby.
- Ask if they prefer large groups to hold their breakfasts during certain times, such as in the later hours of the brunch, or if they want their big-block groups to take up the tables from 8 A.M. to 10 A.M. only. Some sites do specify.

- Ask if there is a separate charge for using a private party room that is next to the brunch area. Again, some sites will charge a room fee of a few hundred dollars, and others charge nothing.
- Ask about pricing for children. Some hotels don't charge anything for kids under ten, others under five years old.

HOW TO PLAN AN AT-HOME BREAKFAST/BRUNCH

- Be sure you will have the time to prepare your breakfast without having to wake up at 5 A.M. to start cooking.
- Allow plenty of volunteers to help you. Friends may offer to bring boxes of donuts or fresh, hot dishes straight from a restaurant or diner.
- Want hot dishes with no fuss? Buy several different kinds of quiches from your grocery store or from a discount store like Costco, and just pop them in the oven for the amount of time listed on the wrapper.
- Use your leftover paper plates, napkins, and cups from your other pre-wedding events such as the bridal breakfast or an at-home rehearsal dinner. If a parent hosted those events at their place, perhaps you could arrange for them to bring those party supplies to your place.
- Judge what you'd need to rent, such as extra chairs, champagne glasses, wine glasses, and tables, and search for the best pricing and quality in town. Arrange with the rental agency to pick up your items a few hours after the party so that you don't have to have a friend key into your home and be there for pickup the following day.
- Floral centerpieces and décor are not needed, but you can have them for free if you arranged to take home some of the floral centerpieces from the wedding itself.

- Be ready for kids' appetites. Buy a few mini boxes of cereals, and set them out with a pitcher of milk and some cut bananas for a kid-friendly breakfast.
- Avoid knife mishaps! Either buy a safe bagel-cutting tool at your home décor store, or have the bagel shop precut your bagels for you.

MENU IDEAS

Some hosts hire professional caterers to bring in hot chafing dishes of the same upscale foods found at that hotel buffet. These are terrific options, depending on what you'd like your morning-after breakfast to be. A stepped-up continental breakfast with an array of bagels and spreads, muffins, breads, fruits, coffee . . . or eggs benedict prepared by a chef wearing a pristine chef's jacket and hat out on your back porch? What can your budget handle?

Some wedding couples pare down other areas of their wedding plans so that they *can* invest more in their morning-after breakfast, surprising guests with a fully catered breakfast alfresco.

- A bagel bar, with six to eight different kinds of bagels and at least three different kinds of spreads: light cream cheese, plain cream cheese, cream cheese with veggies and chives, and so on.
- Want to impress your guests? Warm the bagels and breads in the oven so that they come out restaurant quality, the kind that come in a basket at fine eateries. Make sure your cream cheeses and butters are on the softer side too, for easier spreading. These little details add a lot of impression points to any party.
- Provide smoked salmon for those who like to layer that on their bagels.
- If someone will work the griddle, line up volunteers to carry platters of hot pancakes out to the buffet eight to ten at a time so that they don't get soggy in a bowl.

- Fruit salads are a great idea, especially when you choose in-season, organic fruits cut in creative ways. A customized idea is to set out different types of fruits in different bowls so that guests can choose their own mixes from papaya, grapes, blueberries, raspberries, orange segments, and more. Since some guests can't eat grapefruit due to medicinal interactions, you might wish to keep the different fruits separate.

- Another top trend for your ideal breakfast is setting up a juice bar, including exotic tropical juices like mango and guava juice in addition to orange juice, and adding the interactive element of a yogurt bowl and a blender, plus cut fruit, for those who would like to make their own smoothies.

INSIDE OR OUT? Either at a restaurant or at home, you'll have your choice of indoor or outdoor seating. Both have their upsides (air conditioning vs. cool outdoor breezes), so the main matter for you is determining your style. An outdoor breakfast buffet set up on your terrace might remind you of those fabulous open-air breakfasts served at your favorite tropical resort, so this is one way to give your guests the sense of a tropical getaway without getting on a plane. Just one warning, though: as you see at those tropical resorts, *birds* tend to descend on outside buffets, so don't bring food outside too early, or the songbirds in your yard will steal the party before guests even arrive. Covered platters are an ideal choice for outdoor parties.

INVITATIONS

While you're free to use Evite.com to send out invitations to your breakfast guests, many couples love the chance to create new, themed invitations for this morning-after party. Few want to spend the kind of money they spent on their wedding invitations—which can run into the hundreds of dollars—so they work together to design and print their own. Check back in Chapter 7 for smart budget-saving strategies on these informal invitations.

When it comes to invitation wording, you're free of strict etiquette rules such as having to spell out *Avenue* and *o'clock*. You can get personalized and even humorous with them, reflecting your *breakfast*, your way:

The fun doesn't stop when the reception is over!
Join us for a Morning-After brunch

Westin hotel
Saturday, May 28th
from 8 A.M. to 11 A.M.
Free mimosas! Eggs Benedict! More cake!
It'll be worth waking up early for!
RSVP to Monica and Chuck at 555-8764
by May 12th

OR

Get your breakfast on!
We're not sending you home hungry
after you've traveled all that way to attend our wedding.
We're happy to invite you to a Morning-After Breakfast
at our place,

245 Maple Street
Basking Rock, NJ
May 28th
from 9 A.M. to 11 A.M.
If you show up before 9 A.M., you get to cook!
RSVP to Monica and Chuck by May 12th
555-8764

Another fun concept if you have kids: let *them* be the hosts, and let them design and word the invitations. While you've had so much freedom and fun designing your wedding your way, now it's *their* turn to shine as party hosts. (That stops any parental battles over who gets this party . . . what kind of grandparent would steal a party from a *child?*)

The Day after the Wedding

Yes, for some couples, the festivities of the wedding weekend continue! For many couples whose weddings take place on a Friday night, or even on a Saturday—and for couples who plan destination weddings that bring guests out to an exciting locale for four or five days—the day *after* the wedding is prime time for additional social events. Again, if your friends and family are scattered all over the planet, it may have been ages since you've seen your school friends, and relatives may have flown in from overseas just to be with you at your wedding. You might want to give them even more to enjoy—and get more time with all of them.

> " For us, the day before and the day of the wedding were so packed with activities, and we were running from group to group like excited kids at the wedding itself. It was terrific to see everyone on our guest list, but we wanted more time with them. And they wanted more time with us to make those pricey plane tickets worthwhile. So for those who wanted to stay on throughout the rest of the weekend, we planned a variety of events where it was all about downtime, relaxing cocktail parties, kids-welcome barbecues, you name it. And the memories we made that weekend with our friends and family were amazing. " —*Keira and George*, **newlyweds**

If you were to fly across the country to attend your childhood friend's wedding, and all you got was a few minutes with them at the reception and a few minutes with them at the morning-after brunch, you'd surely wish for just a few more hours of together time. That's what the new trend in day-after events brings you.

Parents can make plans with their own friends, and you can make plans for your own social group. Not everyone has to socialize together on this day, which opens up far more time for you to kick back and relax with the people who helped make you what you are on this day. With the wedding behind you, it's time to uncork a bottle of wine, sit out on the terrace, and hear a ton of great stories about what your groom was like in grammar school. You never knew he was the star kickball player. He never knew you wrote a school play that was performed in front of the entire third grade. And neither of you have met this friend's kids.

Downtime events are obviously tops on most couple's wish lists, with many establishing Open House hours when guests can drop in and take off whenever they wish. Perhaps you live in a fun, touristy town where guests might like to visit the sights on their own, or they might want to spend the morning with their own relatives living nearby. You have one rule: none of these events are mandatory. You're giving your guests the freedom to make their own way.

Very important: don't overbook this day. You don't want to turn into Julie the Cruise Director with your clipboard of activities, asking guests to commit to bocce ball tournaments, tug-of-war competitions, and other events that line up one after the other. A good rule of thumb: plan no more than three events total, and give guests information on nearby attractions they can check out on their own.

This list might be a brochure you pick up at your local tourism office (check *www.towd.com* to locate the one near you), or you might print up a list of your own favorite coffee shops, movie theaters, museums, shopping centers, bookstores, and other day-trip destinations. Just tuck this list in your guests' welcome bags, along with a reminder of the day-after events you have planned, such as a softball tournament at the local park, followed by a barbecue at your place, and a movie or game night at your place—and they're all set. No one needs to dress up. And they know what's on the agenda.

WHO'S HOSTING?

Before we get into the types of events you might want to plan, let's first open this opportunity up to everyone. Parents can host, as can siblings who want to be in charge of an outing or a meal. Favorite aunts and uncles, grandparents, and family friends often open their homes to visiting relatives for a fabulous meal and coffee as the sun sets over their prized gardens. Worried about a relative booking an event at the same time as yours? There's no need to tell Aunt Becky to back off. Guests can choose which event they want to go to, if not both. You're not setting strict rules or claiming the weekend for yourselves. Your laid-back attitude is a gift to your guests and to yourself. How often, after all, do the relatives come to town? Aunt Becky is probably in her glory, polishing her silver and planning to bake her own cake for her party. She gets her soiree her way.

College friends may arrange to hit the nightclubs or the sports bar, or gather at one of their homes, and you're invited to their spontaneously planned outing. There's no rule saying *you* have to plan everything. Most wedding guests tend to group up and make plans on their own, which they will pay for. There's no rule saying you have to pay for *these* extra events, although you're free to if you wish. Your wedding just brought everyone to a central location, perfect for catching up. Guests, then, can make any number of fun group plans with their own downtime or extended stays as well as attending events that you or your parents plan. If you *do* wish to plan day-after events for your guests, here's your guide:

WHAT'S ON THE AGENDA?

You likely have an entire afternoon, evening, and night for events in this day-after events calendar block, so be sure to mix up activities and outings that are appropriate for different times of day—and try to keep drive times to within a half hour, closer if possible.

At Home

You might know your hometown like the back of your hand, but if your wedding will take place in your groom's hometown, your parents' hometown, or at a destination wedding site (even a town just a few hours away from your home, such as wine country or a nearby metropolis), your one-stop-shopping site is the tourism department for that town. Find it through *www.towd.com*, the Tourism Office Worldwide Directory, which will link you to the tourism board of your locale where you'll find listings of museums, theater schedules, shopping districts, and other cool sites, plus valuable coupons for restaurants and tourist attractions. If you call the tourism board, they might hook you up with extra freebies and brochures that make your life easier and your trip more fun.

Here are some activities to consider:

- **Hitting the Road:** Wineries, museums, historic sites, casinos, theaters, family farms during the fall months for apple picking and fall festivals, jazz and art festivals, food festivals, the beach.
- **Sporting activities:** Golf outings, tennis tournaments, horseback riding, mountain biking, white-water rafting, hiking, rock climbing (go to a rock-climbing gym to ensure safety through a harness and profes-

sional guides and instructors), softball games, touch football games, volleyball, bocce ball, horseshoes.

> **"** When I was young, my entire family would have a Labor Day weekend reunion, complete with a softball tournament, a pig roast, and a day of sun and fun. At night, all of the uncles would sit down and have a poker tournament. We haven't had the family reunion in years since everyone lives so far apart now, but we brought back the poker tournament at our day-after celebration as an homage to our uncles, and everyone down to the ten-year-olds played. It was fantastic, even without the dead pig in the yard! **"** — *Eva*, **newlywed**

- **Foodie central:** Culinary tours to the best eateries in town, a tour of your favorite eateries, a trip to your state's People's Choice Award–winning eateries, a trip to the restaurant where you had your first date, ice cream shops, gelato shops, food festivals, shopping trip to your local gourmet market or farmer's market for everyone to load up on fresh, in-season produce, clam bake on the beach.
- **Shopping mecca:** Outlets (visit *www.outletbound.com),* unique boutiques, consignment shop row in expensive neighborhoods, kids' outlet stores.
- **Cultural considerations:** theater productions, free theater in the park, free concerts in the park, festivals, art galleries, museums, kids' museums, aquariums, science centers.
- **Back at home:** Bring everyone back to your place for a day of swimming, sunning, barbecue, and spontaneous competitions in backyard volleyball or Scene It.

At a Destination Wedding

At a destination wedding, you have some amazing day-after events to choose from: scuba diving, horseback riding on the beach, snorkeling, catamaran cruises, cultural tours, hiking through a rainforest with zipline rides across the tree canopy, swimming with dolphins—all exciting adventures that many of your guests have never done before. This too adds to the value of their investment in joining you for your big day, and it presents wonderful photo opportunities for everyone in your group. Outside of island adventure sports and cruises, there's duty-free shopping on many islands, rum-tasting parties, resort-planned theme events like '80s night at the lounge or the spa's special classes and treatments for everyone to enjoy. Your choice of destination wedding locale can fill the entire four or five days for you, with guests possibly getting *free* access to kayaks, free shuttle trips to nearby attractions and other perks they wouldn't get on their regular vacations.

HOW TO END THE DAY

The day-after events provide much-appreciated togetherness, the freedom to wander from event to event, and *your* freedom to rest easy knowing that all your friends and family are well entertained across the grounds of the resort or all across town at friends' and family members' homes. If there's just going to be one afternoon event, after which you—and perhaps your parents—want your privacy, quiet, and an end to the busy weekend, you'll need a great ending point to get guests moving along. There's always that one couple who stays long after the party's over, with hosts needing to put an extra pot of coffee on and bring out more snacks. These lingerers can cause stress when hosts are *done* with the entertaining work and perhaps have hours of cleaning ahead of them.

But how do you get guests to leave without being rude?

As the guests of honor, you can stand up and propose a toast to all who remain: "We're getting ready to take off now, so we thought we'd close down the party with a toast to *you*. We thank you for taking the time and traveling to share this weekend with us, and we wish you all a safe trip home. Cheers!" If you're at your own home, your Cheers are preceded by, "We thank you all for coming, and we're sorry to say we have to shut down the party now. Drive safely, and we'll see you all soon!" Everyone clinks glasses, and the exits begin. This is when the hosts and volunteers can start clearing tables without worrying about looking like they're rushing guests out the door (even though they are!), and when guests get the obvious picture that the festivities are concluded.

After these parties are done, present the hosts with a nice thank-you note, a bottle of wine, a houseplant, or any kind gesture to thank her for her generosity of time and investment in your wedding weekend events. Prep these gifts ahead of time and stash them in your car (if it's a party taking place at a friend's home), or in a separate room from the party taking place at your parents' home. What matters most is that you show you thought about this expression of gratitude beforehand, that you came prepared, and that the day-after event is something you really appreciated. Hosts love the fact that with all you had going on before the wedding, you took the time to thank them with *this*.

Resources

The following list is purely for your research use, and does not imply endorsement or recommendation of the companies or products. Since websites change over the course of time, we some addresses have changed since the time of this printing.

Wedding Planning Websites

Bliss Weddings: *www.blissweddings.com*

Bridal Guide: *www.bridalguide.com*

Brides: *www.brides.com*

BrideTide: *www.bridetide.com*

DIY Bride: *www.diybride.com*

Get Married: *www.getmarried.com*

I Do For Brides: *www.idoforbrides.com*

Martha Stewart Weddings: *www.marthastewart.com*

Pash Weddings: *www.pashweddings.com*

The Knot: *www.theknot.com*

Town and Country Weddings (upscale): *www.townandcou ntry.com*

Wedding Channel: *www.weddingchannel.com*

Gowns

After Six: *www.aftersix.com*

Alfred Angelo: *www.alfredangelo.com*

Bill Levkoff: *www.billlevkoff.com*

Bloomingdales: *www.bloomingdales.com*

Champagne Formals: *www.champagneformals.com*

David's Bridal: *www.davidsbridal.com*

Dessy Creations: *www.dessy.com*

JC Penney: *www.jcpenney.com*

J Crew: *www.jcrew.com*

Jessica McClintock: *www.jessicamcclintock.com*

Jim Hjelm Designs: *www.jimhjelmoccasions.com*

Macy's: *www.macys.com*

Michelle Roth: *www.michelleroth.com*

Melissa Sweet Bridal: *www.melissasweet.com*

Mori Lee: *www.morileeinc.com*

Spiegel: *www.spiegel.com*

Vera Wang: *www.verawang.com*

Watters and Watters: *www.watters.com*

Shoes and Accessories

David's Bridal: *www.davidsbridal.com*

Dyeables: *www.dyeables.com*

Fenaroli for Regalia: *www.fenaroli.com*

JC Penney: *www.jcpenney.com*

Kenneth Cole: *www.kennethcole.com*

Laura Lee Designs*: www.lauraleedesigns.com*

My Little Pretty*: www.mylittlepretty.com*

Nina Footwear: *www.ninashoes.com*

Salon Shoes: *www.salonshoes.com*

Steve Madden: *www.stevemadden.com*

The Pearl Outlet: *www.thepearloutlet.com*

Watters and *Watters: www.watters.com*

Beauty

Avon: *www.avon.com*

Beauty on Call: *www.beautyoncall.com*

Bobbi Brown Essentials: *www.bobbibrown.com*

Care Fair: *www.carefair.com*

Clinique: *www.clinique.com*

Elizabeth Arden: *www.elizabetharden.com*

Estee Lauder: *www.esteelauder.com*

Eve: *www.eve.com*

iBeauty: *www.ibeauty.com*

Lancome: *www.lancome.com*

L'Oreal: *www.loreal.com*

Mac: *www.maccosmetics.com*

Makeover Studio: *www.makeoverstudio.com* (choose your face shape and experiment with makeup shades and looks)

Max Factor: *www.maxfactor.com*

Maybelline: *www.maybelline.com*

Neutrogena: *www.neutrogena.com*

Pantene: *www.pantene.com*

Reflect.com (customized beauty products): *www.reflect.com*

Rembrandt: *www.rembrandt.com*

Revlon: *www.revlon.com*

Sephora: *www.sephora.com*

Jewelry

A Diamond Is Forever: *www.adiamondisforever.com*

American Gem Society: *www.ags.org*

Blue Nile: *www.bluenile.com*

Cartier: *www.cartier.com*

Diamond.com: *www.diamond.com*

Diamond Cutters International: *www.diamondcuttersintl.com*

Ice.com: *www.ice.com*

Jewelry Information Center: *www.jic.org*

Jewelry.com: *www.jewelry.com*

My Little Pretty: *www.mylittlepretty.com*

Paul Klecka: *www.klecka.com*

The Pearl Outlet: *www.thepearloutlet.com*

Tiffany: *www.tiffany.com*

Zales: *www.zales.com*

Invitations

An Invitation to Buy Nationwide: *www.invitations4sale.com*

Anna Griffin Invitation Design: *www.annagriffin.com*

Botanical PaperWorks: *www.botanicalpaperworks.com*

Crane and Company: *www.crane.com*

Evangel Christian Invitations: *www.evangelwedding.com*

Invite Site (made from recycled paper): *www.invitesite.com*

MountainCow: *www.mountaincow.com*

Now and *Forever: www.now-and-forever.com*

PaperStyle.com: *www.paperstyle.com*

Papyrus: *www.papyrusonline.com*

Precious Collection: *www.preciouscollection.com*

PSA Essentials: *www.psaessentials.com*

Vismara Invitations: *www.vismarainvitations.com*

You're Invited: *www.youreinvited.com*

Calligraphy

Calligraphy by *Kristen: www.calligraphybykristen.com*

Petals and Ink: *www.petalsnink.com*

Linens

BBJ Linen: *www.bbjlinen.com*

Chair Covers Online: *www.chaircoversonline.com*

Source One: *www.sourceone.com*

Live Butterflies

Butterfly Celebration: *www.butterflycelebration.com*

Swallowtail Farms: *www.swallowtailfarms.com*

Music and Entertainment

Amazon: *www.amazon.com*

Barnes and Noble: *www.bn.com*

Lyrics Depot: *www.lyricsdepot.com*

Lyrics Freak: *www.lyricsfreak.com*

Music in the Air (New York City area): *www.musicintheair .com*

Piano Brothers: *www.pianobrothers.com*

Romantic Lyrics: *www.romantic-lyrics.com*

Sing 365: *www.sing365.com*

Wedding Channel: *www.weddingchannel.com*

Limousines

National Limousine Association: *800-NLA-7007, www .limo.org*

Flowers and Greenery

About.com: *www.about.com*

Ariella Flowers: *www.ariellaflowers.com*

Botanicals Chicago: *www.botanicalschicago.com*

Floral Design Institute: *www.floraldesigninstitute.com*

HGTV: *www.hgtv.com*

P. Allen Smith: *www.pallensmith.com*

Romantic Flowers: *www.romanticflowers.com*

Sierra Flower Finder: *www.sierraflowerfinder.com*

Favors

Beau-Coup: *www.beau-coup.com*

Bella Terra: *www.bellaterra.net*

Bliss Weddings Market: *www.blissweddingsmarket.com*

Charming Favours: *www.charmingfavours.com*

Cheryl&Co (cookies, brownies, amazing sweets): *www .cherylandco.com*

Godiva: *www.godiva.com*

Illuminations: *www.illuminations.com*

Kebobs.com: *www.kebobs.com*

Lender Ink: *www.lenderink.com*

M&M's: *www.mms.com*

Moma Store: *www.momastore.org*

My Wedding Labels: *www.myweddinglabels.com*

PajamaGram: *www.pajamagram.com*

Pearl River (Asian): *www.pearlriver.com*

Pepper People: *www.pepperpeople.com*

Pier 1: *www.pier1.com*

Surfa's (gourmet food): *www.surfasonline.com*

Wedding Things: *www.weddingthings.com*

Zingerman's (gourmet food): *www.zingermans.com*

Gourmet and Food

Ben & Jerry's: *www.benjerry.com*

Cheryl&Co: *www.cherylandco.com*

Drink Gus: *www.drinkgus.com*

Fizzy Lizzy: *www.fizzylizzy.com*

Food Network: *www.foodtv.com*

Gail Watson: *www.gailwatsoncakes.com*

Personal Chef Association: *www.personalchef.com*

Ron Ben-Israel Wedding Cakes: *www.weddingcakes.com*

Surfas: *www.surfasonline.com*

Steazsoda: *www.steazsoda.com*

Wilton's (cake and cupcake supplies): *www.wiltons.com*

Zingerman's: *www.zingermans.com*

Wine and Champagne

Wine.com: *www.wine.com*

Wine Searcher: *www.winesearcher.com*

Wine Spectator: *www.winespectator.com*

Caterers and Chefs

International Association of Culinary Professionals: *www .iacp.com*

International Special Events Society: *www.ises.com*

National Association of Catering Executives: *www.nace.net*

Personal Chef Association: *www.personalchef.com*

Rentals

American Rental Association: *www.ararental.org*

Warehouse Stores

BJ's Wholesale Club: *www.bjs.com*

Costco: *www.costco.com*

Sam's Club: *www.samsclub.com*

Crafts and Paper

Flax Art: *www.flaxart.com*

Michaels: *www.michaels.com*

My Wedding Labels: *www.myweddinglabels.com*

Office Max: *www.officemax.com*

Paper Access: *www.paperaccess.com*

Paper Direct: *www.paperdirect.com*

Scrapjazz: *www.scrapjazz.com*

Staples: *www.staples.com*

Online Invitations

Blue Mountain Arts: *www.bluemountain.com*

Evite: *www.evite.com*

Hallmark: *www.hallmark.com*

Photo Albums

Adesso Albums: *www.adessoalbums.com*

Exposures: *800-222-4947, www.exposuresonline.com*

Travel

Amtrak: *www.amtrak.com*

ATMS Travel News (adventure getaways): *www.atmstravel news.com*

Charmed Places: *www.charmedplaces.com*

Couples: *www.couples.com*

Expedia: *www.expedia.com*

Hilton: *www.hilton.com*

IberoStar: *www.iberostar.com*

Occidental: *www.occidentalhotels.com*

Palace Resorts: *www.palaceresorts.com*

Porthole Magazine: *www.porthole.com*

Sandals: *www.sandals.com*

SuperClubs: *www.superclubs.com*

Tourism Office Worldwide Directory: *www.towd.com*

Travel and Leisure Magazine (World's Best awards): *www .travelandleisure.com*

Travelocity: *www.travelocity.com*

Travel Zoo: *www.travelzoo.com*

VRBO (vacation house or condo rentals): *www.vrbo.com*

Bed and Breakfasts

Bed and Breakfast Inns Online: *www.bbonline.com*

BnBFinder: *www.bnbfinder.com*

Bed and Breakfast List: *www.bnblist.com*

Hotels.com: *www.hotels.com*

TheInnkeeper: *www.theinnkeeper.com*

Special Event Associations

(find your event planning experts here)

Association of Bridal Consultants: *www.bridalassn.com*

International Special Event Society: *www.ises.com*

National Association of Professional Wedding Videographers: *www.napwv.com*

Professional Photographers of America: *www.ppa.com, 800-786-6277*

Wedding & Event Videographers Association International: *www.weva.com*

Wedding and Portrait Photographers International: *www .eventphotographers.com*

Wedding Officiants: *www.weddingofficiants.com*

Weather and Sunset:

Sunset Time (find the precise sunset time for any day of the year): *www.usno.navy.mil*

Weather Channel: *www.weatherchannel.com*

Additional Sites of Interest:

Art Fool: *www.artfool.com*

Bayley's Boxes: *www.bayleysboxes.com*

Brainy Quotes: *www.brainyquotes.com*

Color Wheel: *www.sessions.edu/ilu/*

Cost of Wedding: *www.costofwedding.com*

Courtship Stories: *www.courtship-stories.com*

Microsoft Office *Live: www.officelive.com*

Personal Stamps: *www.personalstamps.com*

Tableware Today: *www.tablewaretoday.com*

The Wedding Report: *www.theweddingreport.com*

Wedding Details: *www.weddingdetails.com*

Wedding Goddess: *www.weddinggoddess.com*

Wedding Mapper: *www.weddingmapper.com*

Wedding Officiants: *www.weddingofficiants.com*

Wedding Solutions: *www.weddingsolutions.com*

Note from the Author

Congratulations! You're well on your way to planning the wedding you *truly* want, and not the one everyone else wants and expects you to have.

You've done some challenging work as you've read through this book, and you're doing a fabulous job of handling all of the people in your wedding circle. It can be tough to say no to parents, so much so that many brides and grooms out there don't even attempt it. They're just too locked up by their anxieties and fears of not pleasing their parents, or losing their parents' financial contributions to the big day. They just sigh and surrender, watching their wedding dreams float away while everyone else fashions the details of the celebration according to their own plans. Those brides and grooms don't have this book, and *you* are not going to wind up like them—a little bit sad on the wedding day and carrying wounds and regrets into the future. When you think back on *your* wedding, you'll do so with a deep sense of satisfaction that everything went the way you wanted—or better. Everyone had a great time, and the celebration of your marriage was all about the two of you. No anger or resentment for you. Just pure joy that you had the time of your life, spent with the most important people in your life.

It's been my honor and pleasure helping you through this process, and I welcome your questions and stories for upcoming editions of this book. Just write me through my website *www.sharonnaylor.net*, and your success story might be featured!

Enjoy the rest of your planning process, and have a wonderful time on your wedding day—and throughout your wedding weekend!

~ Sharon Naylor

Index